The End of School

To Sharon Warner and Amy Svonavec: the educators who preserved my creativity and ambition from being crushed by the institution of schooling. I am eternally grateful for having had them as teachers during my K-12 education.

TABLE OF CONTENTS

The End of School	9
Acknowledgements	15
WHY HAVEN'T YOU DROPPED OUT OF SCHOOL?	19
Section 1: The Theory of School	51
WHAT IS THE PURPOSE OF CHILDHOOD?	53
WHAT IS CHILDHOOD?	56
LET'S ABOLISH CHILDHOOD	59
HAYEK AND CAMUS WALK INTO A SCHOOL	64
SOME WAYS TO THINK ABOUT SCHOOLING, PART I	70
SOME WAYS TO THINK ABOUT SCHOOLING, PART II: AUTHORITARIAN/LIBERTARIAN	77
A BRIEF DEFENSE OF PLAYING-AS-LEARNING	81
IN PRAISE OF LAISSEZ-FAIRE TEACHERS	85
HOW "BELOW AVERAGE" KILLS DREAMS	87
YOUR HIGH SCHOOL FRIENDSHIPS DIED OUT? REJOICE!	92
Section 2: The Reality of School	97
THE GREATEST LIE WE TELL CHILDREN	99
THERE NEVER WAS A GOLDEN AGE OF HIGHER ED	102
HOW SCHOOLS LIMIT OUR LIVES WITH PERMISSION	108
SCHOOL IS CREATING A GENERATION OF UNHAPPY PEOPLE	113
SOME BAD ARGUMENTS AGAINST HOMESCHOOLING	116
AN OPEN RANT TO THOSE WHO WORRY HOMESCHOOLING DOESN'T PROPERLY SOCIALIZE CHILDREN	122
"WOULD I PUT MYSELF THROUGH THIS?"	132
HIGH SCHOOL IS OVER: SHOULD YOU GO TO COLLEGE?	136
SCHOOLING IS NOT EDUCATION; OR, A LESSON IN STATUS QUO BIAS	144
DO PEOPLE REALLY GO TO COLLEGE FOR AN EDUCATION?	148
THE FALLACY OF "AT LEAST YOU'LL HAVE IT UNDER YOUR BELT!"	150

THE "STEVE JOBS FALLACY" OF OPTING OUT OF COLLEGE   155
HOW COLLEGE BETRAYS OUR BEST STUDENTS   158
YOU ARE NOT YOUR MAJOR   163
THE COLLEGE TRAP AND THE SCHOOLED MIND   166
10 BAD COMMON ARGUMENTS FOR COLLEGE   170

Section 3: Schooling And The Real World   *189*
DESCHOOLING MYSELF   191
THE SCHOOLED MIND   194
THE DESCHOOLED MIND   196
YOU GRADUATED! NOW DESCHOOL YOURSELF   198
DESCHOOLING ISN'T THE OPPOSITE OF STRUCTURE — IT'S THE HEIGHT OF IT   203
YOU ARE NOT A PRODUCT OF YOUR COLLEGE   208
IT'S TIME WE ADMIT THE DEGREE IS SPECULATION, NOT INVESTMENT   214
REQUIRE A DEGREE AT YOUR OWN RISK   221
ERNST & YOUNG DOESN'T REQUIRE DEGREES — WHY DO YOU?   224
DEGREE INFLATION IS OUT OF CONTROL - HERE'S HOW TO FIX THAT   230
WHERE ARE ALL OF THE YOUNG ENTREPRENEURS?   236
ENTREPRENEURSHIP IS THE SOLUTION TO HIGHER EDUCATION -- NOT MORE COLLEGE   249
The End of this Book   *255*

The End of School

Every day of the week for most of the year, millions of young people leave their homes to go to school. They go there to become educated. Millions of public servants devote themselves to the education of these young people in subjects like English, Mathematics, Science, Physical Education, Foreign Languages, and more. These people spend years of their own education learning the best way to sit young people down and have them absorb the information taught at a high enough rate to consider the act of education "successful."

The popular idea behind schooling is simple enough — you take some time away from family to become a socialized, well-adjusted member of society and learn the basics necessary to navigate life. Once you get to a certain age, if you've picked up these basics, you get the opportunity to branch off into something new and exclusive, like medicine, law, accounting, sales, engineering, or any number of other fields. Once you have children, they follow a similar process. You enter into the *educated class* and have new opportunity as a consequence of your schooling.

If young people were merely left alone, their world would devolve into *Lord of the Flies*. They would be mongrels — apt to engage in violence, drugs, useless and destructive vices, and would waste away their youth and grow into unambitious adults. The *un*schooled are the uncontrolled, and the uncontrolled are the uncivilized.

Or so the idea goes.

The reality is quite different. If you're reading this book, I'm sure you've seen plenty of statistics and read stories about how schools fail to meet their goals of providing a quality education to young people. Depending on the country you are reading this in, your own schools surely underperform the schools in other countries on some metric like performance on mathematics exams or reading exams. You've probably read the horror stories of children as young as Pre-K being bullied, beaten, mocked, disparaged, and taught that their self-worth is meaningless by peers and — to everybody's disgust — sometimes even the educators meant to protect them. You probably thought it was odd in the last few paragraphs that I alluded to unschooled young people as those being apt to engage in drugs and violence when it is often the schoolyard where a young person has their first introduction to both of these vices.

People like to focus on these horror stories and examples of education-gone-awry in conversations about education policy. *If only we had more funding for schools, the kids would know how to do long division!* Or *If we had school choice, this wouldn't be an issue in the first place!* Or *It's because of The Department of Education/No Child Left Behind/Common Core that our children are being underserved!* Or pick your pet issue.

These are important points. How schooling is carried out is a vital question that people — especially those who let strangers watch their children for hours every day for more than a decade — *ought* to ask. But these aren't the questions I'm concerned with here. If you want to read a book on education policy reform, go check out that category on Amazon or look up your favorite think tank. I'm sure you'll find something there.

These people leave the very institution of schooling unchecked. They assume that education and schooling are the same thing (or, in more libertarian cases, that schools are probably the best place for education to take place) and don't want to rock the boat about whether we have to take apart the entire idea of school and education in order to get quality education.

The idea at the core of this book is simple: **education and school are not the same thing and they often run counter to each other.** When school and education conflict, education ought to be valued above school. If school is a tool for providing education and it fails to do that, then school, like the hammer that doesn't screw in a nail, should be disposed of in favor of something that *does* get the job done.

Education, then, is the process that every individual has to go through to be equipped with the proper cognitive, philosophical, and physical tools for crafting meaning in the world around them.

We see the need for these tools in quarter-life crises of millennials graduating with multiple degrees after never working a real day in their lives outside of school. These people may be some of the *most schooled ever* (graduating at 24 or 25 after nearly two decades straight of schooling) but fail to lead happy lives because they don't know how to find meaning in the world around them. Despite being years into what we normally call "adulthood," they are children in the existential sense.

They are not victims — nobody forces you to spend decades in school after you turn 18 in the United States — but they are brought up in a culture that places schooling above all else for the ambitious young person.

Thankfully, this can change.

Two vitally important trends put pressure on individuals to take control of education and rip it from the clutches of schooling.

First, the growth of information and the speed at which the world is changing is making it clear that schools can't keep up with the real world's needs. More than 90% of all of the data in existence was created in just the last few years — that's after millennia of data creation. Some of this information is useless and some of it is useful, but the rate at which these two must be parsed apart is moving so quickly that the stodgy, politicized institutions of schools can't keep up with it. Young people at the very best universities are learning outdated ways of coding and doing business that leaves them unequipped for going out at graduation and doing real work. They have to unlearn the bad habits and the outdated ways of doing things in order to pick up new things. Graduation isn't the end of it, either. The successful person today has to constantly be learning, long after they have left school. Add on the cost of schooling (after K-12) and the sheer time it takes and people are caught asking themselves, "isn't there a better way of doing this?"

Second, technology has lowered the cost of access to education and knowledge so monumentally that schools are losing what semblance of a monopoly they held on learning. Knowledge has never been so simultaneously decentralized and centralized as it is today. Decades ago, you would have gone to a library and checked out books, or found a mentor, or re-enroll in university to learn outside of school. Today, you simply google what you want to learn. Udemy, Coursera, MIT Open Courses, Skillshare, and dozens of other platforms provide courses for free or near-free to anybody with access to a computer. Anybody who wants to become well-versed in any subject matter can do so today outside of the university or the school.

What will the end of school look like? I'm not sure. I suspect that as technology further decentralizes education &and knowledge online and lowers the cost to learn new things, traditional schooling will slowly become irrelevant. People will look at schools like they look at the Post Service. "Oh, that thing? I totally forgot it even existed." Some policy revolution may come along and totally change the shape and look of schools.

What I do know is that for the average person, the end of school can't come soon enough. Once we break the stranglehold that the classroom has on education, we open up a universe of new opportunities for learning and living a fulfilled life. The anxiety of school *qua* school that poisons the lives of young people today becomes easier to break down when they understand that education isn't something a bureaucrat controls — it's something only they control.

This book is a compilation of essays and articles that I've written over the last few years while I traveled on my own path from a child of the No Child Left Behind era to the beliefs I hold today. Understanding that education was something only I controlled and that school was often a distraction from equipping myself with the necessities to live a fulfilled life was the most important revelation I've had in my young life.

There is some repetition on themes throughout these pieces. Any piece can be skipped and the next started with ease.

This book is for young people questioning the role of school in education, for parents thinking about how their children will become educated, for educators wondering about the institution in which they work, and for the life-long student looking to stay agile in his thinking. I try to pepper practical advice in with theories on education, entrepreneurship, and ideas for success. The stories and ideas included within are the consequences of hundreds (if not thousands) of conversations I have had with successful entrepreneurs, college opt-outs, my colleagues, intellectuals, and information and knowledge I've picked up through a lot of reading on these topics. Please see the Acknowledgements and the Further Reading sections for specific details.

This is **not** an academic work. I do not try to put together a real philosophy of education in the academic sense of the word — I want this book to be something that anybody making big choices about education can turn to when they need something that can help encourage them or think about the world they are going into. This book is a collection of spontaneous thought, much of which is available at www.ZakSlayback.com, so I have tried to keep original phrasings and wordings where possible. One of the things I set out to accomplish when putting this book together is to show people that you can accomplish big goals like publishing without the permission of others. Go out there and write — if you're saying something worth listening to, people will read it.

Whether or not school comes to an end, you have to take control of your own education. This much is obvious.

Acknowledgements

This book — being largely a compilation of writings over a period of time — is the consequence of conversations, debates, feedback, and inspirations with, from, and by my colleagues, family, and friends. Specifically, Isaac Morehouse helped me push my distaste for standardized K-12 education to its logical conclusions and gave constant feedback along the way. TK Coleman kept me accountable to myself through the writing, compilation, and publishing process of this book. My colleagues at Praxis provide the culture and framework needed to not only carry my ideas out in the world around me but to also provide me with the time needed to put this together.

My intellectual influences are better explained through example in the "Further Reading" chapter, but just a few of the individuals and groups who are most influential in these pages are Peter Gray for his work on the relationship between education, play, and school; John Taylor Gatto for his work on the history of school in the United States and the effects of the institutions on students and teachers alike; Peter Thiel for his work on the importance of monopoly and the dangers of being too "well-rounded"; the Thiel Foundation for the work they do to free ambitious, high-caliber young people from the drudgery of school (and Michael Gibson and Danielle Strachman for their work on building up the Thiel Fellowship and their work at 1517 Fund since then); Nassim Nicholas Taleb for his work on minimizing the downside and the importance of antifragility beyond robustness; John Ramsey and Don Smith for their support of Praxis and the freedom and opportunity it affords me to be able to write something like this; Levi Morehouse for his extremely valuable feedback on the practical psychology of the young entrepreneur; and numerous organizations that support these individuals and others like them. The countless entrepreneurs who gave me their time for conversation over the past few years are many and were indispensable in developing my thought processes here.

Lacey Peace was instrumental through the compilation and publishing process. She compiled, ordered, re-ordered, edited, re-edited, and re-re-edited the chapters of this book, as well as organized the general publication process. This book would not have been possible without her impressive competence, professionalism, and patience.

Alexander Atienza provided the cover design for the book. They say you shouldn't judge a book by its cover, but I encourage it here. This simple design gets across the main points of the book in a way that nearly anybody can understand. His design portfolio can be found here:
http://cargocollective.com/alexanderatienza

School Is Keeping You Down

WHY HAVEN'T YOU DROPPED OUT OF SCHOOL?

I had near-perfect grades through high school, attended my first-choice school -- an Ivy League university -- on a scholarship, worked on a prestigious summer research fellowship, and, had I chosen that route, had the stars aligning to attend a top-tier graduate school. I was far from struggling in my classes -- I had even designed the syllabus with a professor for a majors-only seminar I participated in and went on to take a graduate seminar as a sophomore. I was active on campus, participating in and leading several clubs.

In brief, I was an ideal college student.

Two years in and I dropped out. And this started with asking myself, "Why haven't I dropped out of college?"

A Quick Disclaimer

Before getting into my personal story of leaving school, I want to note that I love learning. Most discussions over the relative value of staying in versus leaving school focus on whether somebody truly values learning. Advocates of the latter allow themselves to be painted as anti-intellectuals, people opposed to the liberal arts, hyper-practical handymen just concerned with what will be marketable in the future. Get rid of that idea right now. Learning and schooling are not the same thing. Sometimes the best learning takes place in school, but that's increasingly not the case when opportunity costs are taken into account. Even more, classroom learning and schooling don't have to be the same thing. You can drop out of college and still enjoy classroom learning. (In fact, you can get the learning for free by auditing classes.)

If you love learning but aren't crazy about school, this chapter is for you.

College Over High School

I enrolled in college, initially, because I wanted to build things. This didn't necessarily mean pursuing a STEM (science-technology-engineering-math) track -- I just enjoyed the process of building, whether simple Legos as a child or organizations and idea-systems as a young adult. College was a step up from rigid high school and appeared to be a prerequisite for any kind of building I wanted to do.

Restless and anxious as a student of the No Child Left Behind-era in public schools, I wondered why we were spending so much time sitting in assemblies about the PSSA (Pennsylvania System of School Assessment) tests and how to properly answer multiple-choice questions when that had no bearing on what I wanted to learn about. Why were we focusing on some ridiculous state-enforced standards that the teachers themselves admitted were totally arbitrary? Why did we take several weeks per year to do these exams? Why were the classes I enjoyed getting cut back for the ones that were enforced through testing regimens? High school became little more than jumping through hoops for state administrators.

School took me away from the learning I wanted to engage in and made me focus on things I didn't want. I loved learning; I just hated school.

I funneled this restlessness and anxiety into a drive to get into college. "I can focus on what I want to learn at college," I told myself. "Once I'm there, I can really get into the weeds of everything I need to know to go out and build what I want to do."

I was mostly wrong.

Once in college the anxiety moved from that which was enforced by school administrators trying to please state education bureaucrats to something less-formally enforced but perhaps more oppressive.

Everybody says that your freshman year is supposed to be uncomfortable. You're supposed to struggle a little trying to find your place at the university, trying to figure out what you really want to do (because, you are told, your major will change several times, so it's silly to be sure of what you want) and who you really are. Your restless desire for definiteness of place and purpose at school will go away, you're assured. (Though this isn't said explicitly, many college students feel this -- that is why they join fraternities, sororities, and clubs at school, and study abroad.) The restlessness from high school wasn't gone, but I just figured it would go away after the first year.

It didn't.

Competition Quashes Progress

Perhaps more alarming was what was happening to my classmates. Many were peers I had met through various activities in high school and who were, at the time, some of the most interesting people I knew. They told me about how they wanted to be entrepreneurs, poets, artists, authors, engineers, and more. They, like me, were going to school as a means to achieving that life for themselves. Still others were generally impressive people who could have achieved anything to which they had fully committed themselves.

These classmates, many of whom had gotten into college with their unique and varied accomplishments, became obsessed with competition, with one-upping each other so they could get the top-tier job or get into the top-tier graduate school. At first glance this should be no surprise, right? Of course students at a top tier school would be competitive. That's what got them in in the first place, right?

Competition isn't an inherently good thing, especially on the individual level.[i] The cult of competition tells us that we have to focus on one-upping each other for a limited set of laurels. At my college it was competition over either pre-professional tracks or graduate-school tracks. Everybody wanted to land the internship with Goldman Sachs or Merrill Lynch. Everybody needed to get the perfect GPA so that he could get into the best medical school. A student at another top-tier school told me that students in her classes would compete to keep their GPAs high so that they could go to "first-page" law schools (meaning, law schools that were on the first page of the US News and World Report rankings).

Competition can be a good motivator if you know why you are engaging in it. If you aren't entirely sure why you are competing, or if your competing is entirely status-driven then competition actually quashes your ability to make personal progress.

To make personal progress you must first focus on what you want to achieve and build plans on how to carry this out. The competitive mindset is the antithesis of this. The difference between the personal mindset and the competitive mindset is where the locus of change sits. In the personal mindset the locus of change is with the individual. If John wants to achieve X, then he must compare himself against what it takes to achieve X and make the proper plans to get there. In the competitive mindset the locus of change is with other people. If John wants to achieve high status at his prestigious university, then he must beat out everybody else. So his plans are determined by what everybody is attempting to achieve.

The great paradox of status-driven competition is that everybody's focus is on everybody else. To get the most out of an elite degree you have to do the most with it. Doing the most with it demands that you do as much as some of the most high-status people who attended the school while not falling behind your peers, who are going for the same thing.

Colleges and universities are breeding grounds for this counter-progressive competitive mindset. By organizing people into peer-groups (graduation classes, schools, majors), schools encourage comparison between students and between achievements. With GPAs determining awards like magna cum laude and admission to prestigious honor societies, college fosters a mindset in which everybody's success is governed by the actions of others.

I saw this mindset capturing my friends and peers. I began to see it creep into my own habits.

"This wasn't how it was supposed to be," I recall telling myself one day. I went to school to escape the competitive mindset of high school. I came here to gain the ability to go out and create the projects I wanted to create. I didn't come here to write papers that could be turned into writing samples for graduate school or entered into competitions with classmates for awards that look great on a resume or that impress a recruiter.

Just Push Through It?

As my sophomore year took off I knew I had to pour my restlessness into something apart from school to prevent falling into this trap. A friend of mine was launching a startup whose mission resonated with me.[ii] I asked if I could pick up some extra work. He wouldn't have to pay me; I would do the work in my free time. It would allow me to pour out my energy without giving in to the temptation to spend that energy competing for top graduate-school slots or places on Wall Street.

The ability to really work on building something outside of an academic context was refreshing, to the point of nearly being a new experience entirely. Like many students, I had spent the last several years putting nearly all my efforts into something related to school. Classes in high school were curated to impress a college-admissions officer. Extracurriculars were a cross-section of what I enjoyed and what would help me with admissions. For the first time in years, I was able to do what I had been working toward this entire time: build something outside of school.

After my sophomore year I was presented with a challenge: I could either finish out my next two years of school while working on the startup and my other goals on the side, or I could go all-in on one or the other. I opted to take a year off and focus on building the startup while pursuing my education myself.

Trying to balance school and a startup would only end in mediocrity. You can't drive a new, radical idea like a startup (especially the kind on which we were working) with your efforts divided, aiming at two different futures. You can't get the most out of your limited and expensive college education by focusing most of your time elsewhere. Trying to juggle both produces mediocre results compared to going all-in on one or the other.

After continuing my work for several months, I was forced to ask myself why I was even in college in the first place. I told myself I had gone so that I could have access to the resources necessary to build projects. But here I was building a project.

I told myself that's what you need to do to get a job. But here I was with a (good) job.

I told myself that's what you need to do to take full advantage of your education. But here I was getting a better education than when I was enrolled as a full-time student.

I told myself that's what you need to do if you want a strong professional network. But here I was with a Rolodex worth more than the entire endowment of the university.

I told myself that's what you do to discover what you want to do. But I knew what I wanted to do since I was a young child, and school just obfuscated that for me. So I dropped out.

What's The Top Idea In Your Mind?

Probably the best part about dropping out was the mental energy that it freed up. Before I dropped out, I told myself I had taken time off to focus on the startup and other projects full-time, but my mind was still ultimately governed by school -- or the eventual need to return.

Y Combinator co-founder Paul Graham has an essay called "The Top Idea in Your Mind."[iii] This is essentially the idea that governs most of your actions. The moment of clarity you have in the shower in the morning, Graham says, is an example of the top idea in your mind.

When you are trying to balance school and an out-of-school project, your project cannot be the top idea in your mind. When school is almost inevitably governed by competition, your own progress cannot be the top idea in your mind. If everything you are doing while on leave or on your gap year is predicated on the belief that you will be returning to school, it cannot receive the benefit of your full attention.

Lots of college students try to launch startups while at school. Some even succeed. But your focus shouldn't be on whether your startup or project is successful for school purposes; rather, it should be on whether it is the best it can be. If you are just running it to pad your resume or to make your time at school seem more impressive, then you are running it for the wrong reasons and should just devote yourself fully to your studies.

(For this reason, I am skeptical of the obsession elite college students have with founding startups. It seems to be another indicator of a growing competitive mindset -- seeping from the university into the startup world, one that has traditionally been defined by a contrarian streak.)

If you want your own personal progress or the progress of your startup or project to be the top idea in your mind, you'll have a very hard time being on leave from school. You'd be best served by dropping out.

So Why Haven't You Dropped Out Of College?

I recount my personal story because it isn't a story of somebody who struggled with school or who went in with a multimillion-dollar idea already rolling. I recount it because I have met hundreds of students in the past several years who feel the same way I did -- anxious, restless, their purpose obfuscated by school -- and because I want to defend the idea that unless you have a very compelling reason to be in college, you are best served by dropping out.

Why do most people go to college?

Middle-Class Mimetics[iv]

Before getting into specific reasons, to understand why most people (i.e., middle- and working-class people) say you should go to college in the United States today, we have to first understand the history of college education and the desire to "be successful."

The idea of achieving success in the United States has, over the last century or so, focused on some conception of "the American Dream." While the stereotype is two-and-a-half kids and a picket fence, as Americans started moving to the suburbs it generally became a struggle for the middle class and the working class to move into the upper-middle class. Those engaged in this struggle found hope in attending college and universities. Spurred by the the postwar GI bill, pundits and politicians alike propagated the belief that a university education would lead individuals and families to prosperity. The successful of the day were likely to have had college educations, making it appear as if a college education was a milestone on the path to success and stability.

All the while, as more people went to college and then into the workforce, the postwar economy started to pick up, not slowing down until the 1973 oil crisis. Baby-boomers grew up during the greatest expansion of the U.S. economy since the Gilded Age, then after many of them got out of college (and after the 1970s disruption), they saw the economic picture brighten once more in the 1980s and 1990s during the Reagan and Clinton eras (culminating in the dot-com bubble of 2001).

The idea that more higher education meant more success was intuitive enough for the boomers and they saw a strong correlation between higher education and economic growth during their lifetimes.

But this gets the process wrong on both counts.

Universities and colleges weren't causes of aristocracy and wealth; they were products of aristocracy and wealth. Aristocrats didn't send their children to universities to make sure they got the tools necessary to stay aristocrats -- they sent them because it was essentially several years of leisure and only the most well-off could afford such a lifestyle.

The university was never intended to train people for high-wage jobs or to lift them up the economic ladder. At best it was an institution to train the clergy in the Middle Ages and then academics in the industrial age. This is why liberal-arts schools place such heavy emphasis on academic subjects -- they were designed to create professors.

As global wealth increased through the Industrial Revolution, aristocrats who were already comfortable in their wealth had two options for their children who were coming of age: A) send them to work, or B) give them some leisure among their same class. The university evolved into an institution to help young aristocratic men to transition into adulthood by moving away from home and studying subjects only the most well-off had the leisure to study. The backgrounds of elite American universities make this obvious. Princeton has "eating clubs"; Penn has "the

Philomathean society"; and Yale's secret society culture is a relic of this era.

This isn't a conspiracy. It's simply saying that the universities were never intended or designed for the use to which Americans of the mid-20th century put them. Agricultural schools of the antebellum era did start training people in practical trades, but even their growth was ill-suited to preparing people to create value in order to climb the economic ladder.

The postwar boom that the baby-boomers experienced in their youth was also not a product of a more-educated workforce. Immense technological growth from World War II, the rise of the semiconductor and information theory, and artificial growth stimulated by the Marshall Plan in Europe and American efforts to rebuild Japan were more likely causes of this long- and short-term growth. In other words, the gears of economic progress were in motion long before the boomers were even born, let alone before they attended school. PayPal co-founder, Peter Thiel, notes in *Zero to One:*

> Whether you were born in 1945 or 1950 or 1955, things got better every year of the first 18 years of your life, and it had nothing to do with you. Technological advance seemed to accelerate automatically, so the Boomers grew up with great expectations but few specific plans for how to fulfill them.... Since tracked careers worked for them, they can't imagine they won't work for their kids, too.[v]

The myth that more formal schooling means more success is exactly that -- a myth. The United States is a culture that has been built by those who didn't wait for four years before taking on life: Thomas Edison, Cornelius Vanderbilt, Andrew Carnegie, John D. Rockefeller, Henry Ford, Mark Twain, Frank Lloyd Wright, Howard Hughes, Buckminster Fuller, Larry Ellison, Bill

Gates, Steve Jobs, James Cameron, Travis Kalanick, Mark Zuckerberg, and Harrison Ford are just a few examples.

That smarter people, on average, tend to go to college today, or that people with higher pay, on average, went to college can be explained by a simple selection bias. The cultural mythos we build around college propels smarter people and those more likely to achieve high pay in life (these are not always the same thing) along this path. They likely would have been successful without college.

With names like those above, why don't you start asking yourself, "Why haven't I dropped out of school?"?

A Disclaimer: Don't Be Cheetos-Dude

Before looking at the reasons that might be holding you back from dropping out of college, I want to issue a quick disclaimer: dropping out of school is traditionally maligned because the alternative in most people's minds is to become "Cheetos-Dude." We all know Cheetos-Dude. He's the slacker who sits at home eating junk food and watching television when he has work to do. He's the guy who dropped out of college because it was too hard for him. He has a dead-end job because he's not willing to put in the work he needs to get a better job.

If you want to be Cheetos-Dude, by all means go ahead. This chapter isn't for you, though.

If you want to be more than Cheetos-Dude -- if you feel like you see Cheetos-Dude all over your college campus, like you've been cheated by the college mythos, like you might be able to do more with the freest years of your life -- keep reading.

The best way to prove a stereotype wrong is to live differently.

"I'm not like those you named."

Naming industrial titans, famous actors, and the men who built Silicon Valley isn't entirely fair, and it is exactly what the culture that glorifies college propagates. Like only those rare geniuses can go without. Maybe you thought about dropping out of college, but thought to yourself, "Yeah, but I'm not Steve Jobs or Mark Zuckerberg," or you had a family friend tell you, "Yeah, it made sense for them, but you aren't them!"

Get that idea out of your mind entirely. It's absurd, unfair, and not constructive.

At it's core this is a double standard. It's a double standard that tells college dropouts, "You won't be successful unless you reach the status of the megasuccessful." Even more egregiously, it tells them, "If you aren't successful, you have nobody else to blame but yourself because you decided to drop out of college." It overlooks everybody else who didn't go to college and are moderately successful (and also forces somebody else's definition of success on you, but that's another topic entirely). It overlooks the college dropout who is just as successful as the banker down the street, the engineer next door, or the teacher one block over.

Nobody tells the college graduate, "You better be as successful as [the president of the United States, the chairman of Goldman Sachs, the CFO of Deloitte]! If you aren't as successful as [arbitrary standard I choose], then you have nobody else to blame but yourself because you decided to go to college!"

You don't need to be a Steve Jobs or a Mark Zuckerberg or a Harrison Ford to drop out of school. You don't need to abide by the double standard of the mythos built up and enforced by the boomers against their children. For every not-Steve Jobs or not-

Mark Zuckerberg, there are dozens of not-Barack Obamas or not-Larry Pages. Next time you are hit with this justification for not dropping out, just flip the script.[vi]

"I need a job."

If you ask most people why they went to college, they will likely tell you that it was so they could get a job. They didn't necessarily know what job or even what kind of job they wanted, but they just knew that they should go to college if they wanted to get a job.

This is absurd -- although not entirely their fault, considering how much teachers, parents, and guidance counselors probably pushed the "you need a degree if you want a decent job" dogma on them.

Going to college to study an indefinite field to get an indefinite job for an indefinite future sets the building blocks for an indefinite life. Going to college without knowing what you want to get out of it or what kind of job you want to land just sets you up for not being in the driver's seat of your own life.

If you are sure of what you want to do and absolutely need a degree to do it (which pretty much just leaves lawyers, doctors, and academics), then go for it. But if you aren't sure, going "just because" sets a dangerous precedent for your own life.

That might sound like high-level abstract talk but the idea that you go to college to get a job is absurd on the ground-level, too.

Employers who require college degrees don't do it because they necessarily think that those with college degrees are more likely to be valuable employees. Instead, this hiring practice is a relic of the pre-Internet era. It's an HR-move that helps companies sort out applications that are more or less likely to be worth looking at. If you were hiring in 1990, when college graduates were much fewer and when there was really no other way to verify a candidate's basic abilities like writing and showing up to work, a degree might have told you much more.

If you're hiring in 2015, when degrees are a dime-a-dozen and when Google is at your fingertips, college tells you considerably less about a candidate. It doesn't do a great job of sorting high-value candidates from low-value candidates when Jack, who showed up to class twice-per-semester and was always hungover, has the same BA as Sally, who showed up every day and never went out during school.

Richard Bolles's perennial bestseller, *What Color Is Your Parachute?*, goes through the basic steps for getting hired in a changing economy. Recent editions have included a chapter called "Google Is Your New Resume." What Bolles gets at here isn't that you need to be careful with what you post on social media, but rather that your entire portfolio of work is now available with a simple Google search of your name. If you want to be known as a designer, you can put up a site showing off your design work. If you have done sales, you can upload your sales decks to Slideshare. If you want to show off all your work generally, LinkedIn is the fastest-growing professional network in the world.

"Yeah, but lots of companies require BAs to get hired."

The BA requirement just shows that a candidate is a minimally viable candidate. It doesn't say anything else. A strong set of work experiences or a record of having created value in the marketplaces shows more than a BA does.

Many employers are changing their hiring copy slightly in light of degree-inflation. "BA or equivalent work experience" has started appearing on the websites of those who do require BAs. CEOs and hiring managers tell me this is because they realize the degree doesn't teach more than what some time in the field can teach.

Even more, degree requirements are disappearing entirely for companies born in the digital era or those trying to keep up with digital-era companies. Uber -- founded by UCLA dropout Travis Kalanick -- is a $51 billion company (at time of writing) that employs full-time business people, customer experience agents, and software engineers on every continent. Uber does not require a degree for many of their business positions.

"Okay, well, I'm going to figure out what I like and want."

Going to college to "discover yourself" or to "figure out what you want from life" are common reasons given by those who want to encourage more young people to attend. This overlooks a few facts:

1) This is a very expensive way to figure out what you want.
2) This is a very time-consuming way to figure out what you want.
3) This isn't a very good way of figuring out what you want.

College is expensive. Everybody knows this. I don't have to type out the statistics on the average cost of a four-year undergraduate education here because it has been repeated so often it is almost cliche. It's easy to say "College is a great way to discover yourself!" when you aren't footing the bill.

And even if you don't have to pay a hefty price tag for four years of college experience, it's still four years of your life. The opportunity cost of college -- or the cost of all those activities that are forgone by spending your time in college -- is mind-bogglingly high. Recall the "equivalent work experience" requirement from above. That, if not more, is the opportunity cost of college.

Bill Gates returned to Harvard for a semester after launching Microsoft. If he had stayed in school instead of going back to Microsoft, his opportunity cost would have been the creation of all the wealth and value his tenure at Microsoft produced, and he would probably be considerably worse off for it.

The idea that college is a good place to figure out what you want is deeply flawed because it is an environment and institution almost entirely isolated from the real world, without real consequences for failure or success, and without real incentives (i.e., prices, profit, loss) influencing it.

To get an accurate picture of what you want from life (i.e., the time you spend in the "real world"), you are best served by spending time in the real world. If you are like I was and are coming out of 12 years of compulsory schooling, you probably don't have a good idea of what the real world is like. Your past decade-plus has revolved entirely around school and what comes after school.

The best argument I've heard for using college to figure out what you want is that it provides a safe environment for you to try out different things and fail at them. If you fail and fall, you won't fall that far and you can get right back up and try something else, the argument goes.

But even this defense assumes too much of college. For many students, failure at school is tantamount to failure at life. Even those with a strong individualistic streak find themselves comparing their relative success in school to that of their classmates. They identify their success in life with their success as a student.

Failing at something in the real world isn't entirely bad, either. Most successful entrepreneurs fail at several ventures before they succeed. Most successful artists are rejected many times over before they get their break. Experiencing failure in the real world (and not the sanitized version of it found in college) might be good for many people, so long as they have the resolve to rebound from it. Attempting to avoid failure also puts a creative strain on the individual and provides an incentive to create and innovate in ways that would be difficult without this incentive.[vii]

"I want higher pay."

"Studies show that going to college increases lifetime earnings by $1,000,000!"

You've likely heard this line repeated by pundits or high school guidance counselors. The message is clear: if you want higher pay, go to college.

But these kinds of studies are subject to a very strong selection bias.

The type of person who was more likely to attend college in 1990, 1995, or 2000 (the earliest time frames you could use for projecting lifetime earnings) is probably somebody who was moderately middle class, moderately intelligent, and moderately competent, at least. This person is then compared with the average student in the same age range who decided not to go to college – a less-impressive individual. The first person would have likely succeeded whether or not he went to school!

For a full analysis of earnings in light of schooling, researchers would have to follow twins from birth, making sure they had the same IQ and competence when they graduated high school. They would have to control for every variable influencing the individual's decision to go to college. No such study has been done.

The same kind of statistical logic can be used to justify going to an elite college over an average college, except here the poor logic has been hit with counter-studies.[viii] Turns out that people who attend elite universities aren't necessarily going to earn more than their peers at average universities *because earnings are more than a reflection of education status.*

Recall what I said about the degree being a sorting mechanism for hiring. At one time this was also the case for giving raises, especially at the executive level. Getting an MBA would always be justified because it would bring a raise. As more people get MBAs and as more ways of comparing candidates arise, this is no longer the case. What was once considered a no-brainer is now highly contentious. What has happened to the MBA is an omen for what is going to happen (and is starting to happen) to the BA.

"I need a network."

College is said to be one of the best places to develop a network and get to know people who can be professionally helpful later in life. Whether it's a fraternity brother with business connections you can call on for your jobseeking son or a classmate that you decide to co-found a business with, colleges have traditionally been hubs of networking gold.

But is it the best place to acquire a network?

As a young person, the most valuable kind of network you can acquire is one that is vertically diverse. This is a network with lots of different people who are at more advanced stages of their careers than you. These are people who have built up social capital and are willing to go to bat for you when you most need somebody to go to bat for you. These are people with reputations and connections who are willing to listen to you. They're how you will most likely get your first job or two and how you will propel yourself forward. They're the ones who can connect you with VIPs (e.g., celebrities, investors, potential mentors).

The best way to actually acquire a vertically diverse network is to go out and work somewhere. Working at a high-growth startup is one of the best ways of doing this because it is high-risk and high-reward. If the startup succeeds, you gain the connections and laurels of being on a successful team. If it fails, you have at least gained the professional connections of those who joined you.

College provides you with lots of people at the same stage of life as you, although they might have different interests and backgrounds. As you get older, you will likely diverge a little, but not terribly. You'll stay in the general professional range as most of your peers. Your strongest connections will be with those in your immediate social circle, then your major, your school, your university, and your interests (e.g., sports, competitive clubs, etc.), in descending order. You may meet a few alumni, and you'll know some professors, but they'll be outside your field and won't be of much help to you after you graduate unless you pursue a career in academia.

A horizontally diverse network can be useful, for sure -- the PayPal mafia primarily went to two different schools and were almost all in the same age range -- but it isn't as powerful as a vertically diverse network for early professional life.

The best way to acquire a powerful professional network is to put some skin in the game and go out into the professional world.

"I need social interaction."

"The college experience" has become synonymous with everything from branching out into new social circles to reenacting *Animal House* every other weekend. Despite what liberal-arts professors will declare every year in articles at *Inside Higher Ed* and the *Huffington Post*, college is, for many students, a consumption good. They're looking to get a certain experience out of college and are paying for that experience. Especially if you come from a more limited upbringing or social background, the idea of going to a university and getting to know different people with a plethora of backstories can be exciting.

Just like the professional network, we have to ask ourselves if this is the best way of acquiring this experience.

Want to know how you can get the college experience without all the debt and opportunity cost? Just move to a college town and participate in intramural clubs and competitions. Plenty of people do this. They either move there hoping to become students someday but never enroll, or simply go for a few years to experience the life and culture with no intention of enrolling. It's an easy way to get a big part of why most people attend school in the first place.

But maybe you aren't just looking for the parties and the sporting events. Maybe you're looking to expand your social networks and looking for new experiences.

If you're a bright, driven young person, it isn't easy to go out and meet new people, especially if you are forced to do so through some other obligation. School forces us to meet each other by placing us within certain social confines. Work can do the same. Joining a high-growth team that requires a dynamic young worker is one easy way of expanding your social networks. Another is actually forcing yourself to meet people.

In *The Four Hour Workweek,* Tim Ferriss challenges readers to ask for the phone numbers of several strangers of the opposite sex. Even if you aren't actually interested in dating them, he says, asking for their numbers will make it much easier to initiate conversations elsewhere in life. Putting yourself outside your comfort zone allows you to shed the self- and otherimposed blinders that keep you from realizing just how easy many supposed difficulties are to overcome.

So go out there and try meeting four new people, using nothing but looks alone. You'll be astonished at how easy it is. Even if you get rejected, you'll learn through failure how to adapt your ways.

"What if I just want to learn?"

Let me be clear: I am not opposed to education. It is my love of education that drove me away from school. In a culture as thoroughly schooled as modern America, where most everybody has gone through compulsory K-12 education and more are going through seemingly compulsory college education, it can be difficult to differentiate between "education" and "school." It can be even harder to differentiate between "school" and "classes."

Not all education is schooling, and not all classes are schooling. For some people, classes are the best way to learn, but this doesn't mean they have to be enrolled in school in the traditional sense. For many, education and schooling are at odds with each other, with schools designed to produce a different result than what the individual wants to get out of his education.

If you are looking at staying in school because you want an education, you again must ask yourself, "College compared to what?"

You need not be a radical autodidact to find that school does a terrible job educating. From social pressures to majoring in "marketable" subjects to putting assignment minutiae before learning as a whole, schools create and reinforce incentive systems that make it difficult to focus on education first and foremost.

The great thing about the rise of the Internet is that it has lowered the barrier to entry for so many fields. Your cell phone has more human knowledge available to it than all of the libraries of Harvard circa 1960. You just have to find a way to sort out that knowledge. This is what MOOCs (Massively Open Online Courses) like Coursera try to do. By having experts sort through and organize the available knowledge in a variety of fields, MOOCs make education open to anybody with an Internet connection. With degree-mills like the University of Phoenix taking advantage of this technology, "online education" gets a bad rap. People imagine somebody who didn't have what it takes to get into a "real college" sitting at home and doing their courses in their underpants. Whether this reputation is deserved is beside the point. What matters is this: if education matters to you, can this serve as a viable alternative?

Possibly so.

But one of the claimed advantages of college is that it allows you to focus on studies and nothing else. You can be a student full-time and not have to worry about paying the bills or going to work, the story goes.

This might be the case, but that doesn't mean it is desirable. Education and work shouldn't be easily divisible. Creating and enforcing an artificial barrier between the two just distances education from its application to our lives and makes us view work as a mere necessity. Both education and work are necessary and both have major impacts on how we structure our lives.

Balancing work with education makes it harder to compartmentalize both, allowing for applications from one to travel to the other. Studying Bertrand Russell's philosophy of work can be great when you aren't working, but it can have life-altering impacts when you are working. Getting a good grasp of economics can appear valuable in the abstract, but it can mean the difference between staying in your current job and launching your startup when you are working.

It's time that we rethought the idea that education and work are to be divided. We get the most out of both when we experience them concurrently.

For some people academia is the best place both to learn and work, and they feel comfortable in school. If you are still reading this chapter, you probably aren't this kind of person (or you have a morbid curiosity of why people want to tell others it is okay to leave school). If you are this kind of person, great! You'll do great in school. Go become a professor. Just don't tell others they have to follow your path.

"My parents won't let me drop out."

Parents of young people are some of the most ardent believers in the American collegiate mythos. They saw progress happen as more people got college degrees. They saw their friends go off to college and come back to phenomenal jobs. They saw college *work*.
Or so they thought, at least.

Even if college was the ideal way for a young person to take control of his life in that generation, this doesn't mean that it would be for a later generation. Like every generation before them, the boomers are afraid to let their children participate in something they -- the parents -- view as risky.

Their objections are motivated by love and concern -- but they don't have to constrain you.

One of the best ways to prove to your parents that you will not fail to achieve anything or be motivated in the real world is to take a leave of absence from school. Take a semester or a year off; get a job at a fast-growing company; find a mentor; or travel the world successfully and show them that you can not only take care of yourself outside of school, but you can flourish while doing that. Once you do this, their resolve will likely weaken, and you will be able to convince them more easily that you should drop out.

If they're still adamant, and you are sure you want to drop out, go ahead and do it anyway. Don't do it to be hostile or confrontational with your parents. Do it to show them that you are behind your commitment 100 percent. Do it to show them that while you respect their opinions, you can think for yourself. Do it to enforce your ownership rights over your own decisions. Even if they are upset and angry in the moment, they're likely to come around as you flourish without school.

"I want to drop out. I just don't know where to start."

Okay, you're ready to get started, but you don't know where to turn. You may not have a mentor you can call on immediately to ask for a job, or you don't have your own idea that you can launch.
That's okay.

Getting started is hard. Just as in physics, an object at rest requires action by an outside force before it starts moving. Once you start moving, you'll be astonished at how easy it is to keep moving.

If you're looking to drop out and take control of your education and your career, but don't have a project to jump into immediately, your first goal should be identifying something you think you would enjoy. But how do you know what to pick?

Think about the things you *hate*.

Now think of all the jobs you could work in where you would be doing those things you hate as seldom as possible.

Find a company near you that you think does something interesting and inspirational, a company for which you would be happy to wake up in the morning and go to work. Find the highest-ranking person in that company and write an email explaining your background, experience, and reasons for wanting to work there.

Make your request clear: let me work for you.

If you must work for free first, do it (see below). Even if it is just a few hours per week, working for free and doing good work will not only ingratiate you with the team but it will also put them in a position where, as time goes on and your opportunity cost rises with your increasing skill and experience, the company will be forced either to offer to pay you or find a replacement for you. Turnover costs are high, especially at startups, and replacing good talent is incredibly difficult even at entry level. Making yourself indispensable is your first step towards landing a job.

But how to make yourself indispensable? If you've been in school your entire life, you probably lack even the most basic workplace skills. How are you supposed to compete with people who might have more experience, connections, or a degree?

The most valuable skill is basic competence.

From executive vice presidents to summer interns, organizations often have a difficult time finding people who will do what they say they will do, show up when they say they will show up, and do their work well.

If you can approach your work singlemindedly for a short period of time and make yourself indispensable, you'll never have a hard time getting a paid fulltime job.

If you have a skill, especially one in high demand like coding, sales, or a trade, simply make that clear when you email someone about work.

"But what if I don't get a reply?"

Be persistent. Send an email every week insisting on an interview and emphasizing that you can prove your worth. Worst-case scenario? You don't get a reply and learned how to be persistent in emails. Best case? You land the job.

Send emails to several companies. Showcase your work. Make your request clear. Don't ramble about different things you could do. Ask if you can work with them.

This will be your first step towards escaping school and being in the driver's seat of your education and career.

A Modest Proposal

Every year thousands of families will open up their pocketbooks and tap into the sacrosanct savings fund that many parents set up before their first child was even born: the college fund. As they prepare to send their high school graduates off to college, they'll shell out thousands of dollars to universities, companies, and textbook publishers — maybe symbolically giving the money to the student first, but with the clear understanding that it can then only be given directly to the universities. This money will support the student through the college years and help him launch himself forward into stable adulthood, offsetting any student loans he may need and making life a little bit easier.

Perhaps more romantically, the money is to provide the young person opportunity. Any good parent wants to give his children the opportunity to become their best possible selves. The most obvious and safest path to this in the mind of the boomers is to attend college. Go and learn about the world for a few years; try something new; and at the very least, even if you don't find a job on graduating, *you'll have a good experience and a degree under your belt.*

But this is the romanticized vision of the college experience. As I've said, in a world of *so much more information*, so much more (*cheap!*) connectedness, and *generally more opportunities for ambitious young people*, there's a huge opportunity cost to just taking the college-as-success pill no-questions-asked.

But even more, there's the huge financial cost to the college savings fund. If the purpose of saving up so much money ($10,000, $20,000, $50,000, maybe upwards of $100,000) is to use it so that your child may learn how to become a successful adult and be exposed to the experiences that will mold him as such, giving that money directly to a college is one of the worst possible things you could do.

Imagine that rather than giving this money to a university to cover tuition, parents instead took the money and gave it to their child as a "coming-of-age fund." The stipulations are simple: the newly christened adult can spend it on whatever he would like. If he wants to spend it on college, he is free to do so. But he is also free to spend it on a fancy car, a down payment on a house, traveling around the world, or seed-funding his own company. It would give him the freedom to explore his options without feeling pigeonholed.

Would some people take the money and blow it? Absolutely. Would others make something greater out of it than if they had spent it on college? Absolutely. What matters is that these young adults would actually be treated as adults and given the freedom and responsibility to deal with freedom and responsibility.

Even in the worst-case scenario, where a young person blows the money on sheer thrills and gambling, he would still learn more about himself and about managing money than if he were subsidized to sit in an academic bubble for four years, where he rarely felt the pain of spending $10,000 per semester so the university vice provost to the assistant secondary dean of diversity student life could afford a new Mercedes-Benz.

The college savings fund appears to be a great idea in the abstract — a sort of safety net to help push children of boomers onto the path to the middle class — but when considered with the opportunities it closes off and the other ways the money could be spent, it is a vestige of a risk-averse generation. Giving young people the opportunity to spend large sums of money however they wish would teach them more about themselves, the world around them, and the opportunities they do and do not have better than going to college simply because that's what they've been told to do.

You Do You

Ultimately, the decision to drop out of school is a highly personal one, which can be fraught with waves of emotions thanks to a culture that glorifies the collegiate experience. I did not write this chapter to convince you to drop out of school if you love school. I wrote it for the people who, like me, feel that they can get something more out of the best years of their lives. I also wrote it because the cultural narrative around school is mind-bogglingly unfair. If you announce you are going to college, not a person will tell you to check yourself and make sure you aren't making a rash decision. If you announce you're going to drop out of school, you'll get stern talking-to from your parents and an email from your aunt you haven't seen in years; your friends may refer you to the school therapist. I want to flip that narrative.

Be very discerning about what you do while you are young. Being 18-25, with little debt, no mortgage, and no strong familial commitments gives you a level of freedom that very few other people have. You can try many things, take many risks, put a lot on the line without losing too much.

Leaving school isn't easy, and it is different depending on where you live. Being a dropout in Silicon Valley isn't as interesting as being one in Pittsburgh, Pennsylvania. People may discount you. People may not care. Prove them wrong. Make them esteem you by doing good work.

Section 1: The Theory of School

We destroy the love of learning in children, which is so strong when they are small, by encouraging and compelling them to work for petty and contemptible rewards, gold stars, or papers marked 100 and tacked to the wall, or A's on report cards, or honor rolls, or dean's lists, or Phi Beta Kappa keys, in short, for the ignoble satisfaction of feeling that they are better than someone else.

John Holt

WHAT IS THE PURPOSE OF CHILDHOOD?

The average child spends eight-to-ten hours in school every day of the week — getting up before dawn, standing in the cold, getting on a bus, and sitting through learning materials that have been pre-determined to be necessary for their success as students. The average American elementary schooler spends 934 hours in school per year,[ix] and many spend much more time at boarding schools, after school programs, and after-school detention and suspension.

To what end?

Why do we spend so much time, money, and resources on schooling? And why do we make it compulsory for children to attend a pre-approved schooling system?

"Well that's obvious, it's so they can be educated."

But educated *in what*? If we allow the assumption that schooling = education (which we ought not to, but will for sake of argument here), then the content of what the schools teach is going to determine in what the children are educated. If schools teach math, then children will become educated in math, for example.

"Educated in the skills and knowledge they need to know to be successful."

This yet again raises another question: successful *at what*? Life is complex and people set different ends for themselves. Sometimes (oftentimes?) they just accept the ends that they find themselves wanting without much critical reflection. There's no common definition for what it means for children to be "successful."

"Obviously what we mean is that we want them to have the skills and knowledge necessary to become successful adults."

Giving young people the cognitive and educational resources they need to "become successful adults" is a noble end. It is an incredibly haughty and presumptuous goal, though. What does it mean to "become successful adults?"

There are libraries full of books by philosophers reflecting on what the purpose of life is and what it means to be fulfilled and successful for adults. If childhood is defined by schooling, and if schooling is defined by the ability to become a fulfilled/successful adult, then childhood is defined by the ability to become a fulfilled adult. The problem is, *nobody knows what this means*, and *even if they did, it is different for everybody*.

The absurdist philosopher Albert Camus wrote in *The Myth of Sisyphus* that there is no objective meaning to life. Life is, in Camus's words, absurd. We have to come to grips with this fact and create *our own meaning* from this lack of meaning. Only when we can delight in this fact can we find our own drive and fulfillment. To assume that this is the same for all the students in a classroom, let alone all the subjects of the federal Department of Education, assumes that there is a standard by which one can create meaning from the absurd.

If the point of childhood is to become a successful adult, then we should be even more opposed to standardized schools. The ability to craft meaning and fulfillment from the world is something that is unique for each individual person and can only be crafted through experience with and interaction in the world. The point to childhood is no different than the point to adulthood: there is no point. The point is to find meaning and fulfillment for ourselves. This is a deeply personal and subjective experience, and one that cannot be taught via scantron bubbles and school-wide textbooks.

WHAT IS CHILDHOOD?

Since childhood, and the purpose to which it is oriented via education and schooling, is defined in terms of success at adulthood, and since success at adulthood is something we cannot define, childhood has no definite purpose. The purpose of childhood is the same as the purpose of adulthood: to find meaning and fulfillment in the world.

This leads to another important question: *what is childhood?* Generally, childhood is defined in terms of two things:

1) Not being adulthood
2) Being a student

On the first point, children are thought as non-adults. They don't possess the rights of adults. They don't possess the social standing of adults. They don't possess the command of adults. They don't even possess the social respect of adults (listen to how adults speak to children, and then how they speak to cognitively-impaired adults).

But defining an idea or concept in terms of its negative is rarely fruitful since it leads us to then have to define the negative. Rather, we should focus on childhood as "being a student."

Some critics of standardized, traditional schooling regimes have argued that compulsory schooling extends childhood beyond its natural range. By requiring that young adults attend school until at least the age of 18, we infantilize them and subjugate them to the whims of people just a few years older than them. They conceptualize that their agency is not something they actually possess until the end of the legally mandated schooling regime.

Strong social pressures to enroll in higher education then extend this infantilization. Young adults, upwards of 21, 22, or 23, are now subject to the arbitrary rules and expectations of universities and colleges that they have very little choice in whether or not they attend. While they are not *legally* mandated to attend college, the social pressure from friends, family, and low interest rates encouraged by the government make it hard to say no.

So, childhood arguably ends somewhere between ages 18 and 23 on the second conception.

Why should childhood even be a concept in our minds? We have to legally have some form of status for persons who cannot make fully-informed decisions for themselves, but how much of this status as a person who "cannot make fully-informed decisions for themselves" is reality and how much of it is reinforced by telling children they don't know what they need to know until ages 18-23?

If the purpose of childhood is the purpose of adulthood — to find fulfillment and craft it in the world — then why artificially divide life into two stages? Why not just conceive of children as little adults — persons to interact with the world and learn new things about it in the same way that the 21 year old who is just now figuring out how to replace a halogen light bulb in their car does?

This artificial division only delays the necessity to confront the reality that life has no definite purpose outside of what the individual crafts for it (whether that be religious, spiritual, entrepreneurial, intellectual, artistic, or any combination does not matter). We owe young persons something better than the infantilization brought with the concept of childhood.

LET'S ABOLISH CHILDHOOD

Childhood is a stage of life primarily defined by being a student in most developed nations. While the concept has at least three components — legal (i.e., being less than 21 years of age in most states in the US), biological (i.e., being at a stage when most of the body is still developing — until about age 26), and social (i.e., studentdom) — its social component is the one by which we *think* of most children.

Childhood-as-studentdom

When an adult thinks of a child, what thoughts come to mind? Summer vacation, getting on and off a school bus, going to take exams at school, preparing to get into college, taking a driver's ed class, and recess are probably some of the most common thoughts. The common theme that ties these thoughts together is schooling. Schooling is the primary defining characteristic in the common conception of childhood. This brings with it all the baggage that schooling does. This conception has children subservient to adults, naturally unfocused and oriented towards play, and requiring structure and authority imposed upon them.

Adulthood, on the other hand, is seen as "not-childhood." It is a place that adults commonly refer to as "the real world," — as if the world children occupy is somehow artificial (and it may be in schools) — with "real skills" and doing things that commonly fall into two categories of "work" and "recreation" or "leisure." Adults are charged with the task of not only supporting themselves and their kin, but also to craft meaning for themselves in a world in which they have long neglected the question. It may come at a quarter-life crisis after college, or a mid-life crisis upon reaching the "dream" and seeing mortality for the first time on the horizon, but at some point many adults confront themselves with the question of what the meaning of life is.

The childhood-as-studentdom conception exacerbates this problem for adults. As adolescents and young adults, they see themselves as in a developmental stage. Their goal as children/adolescents/young adults is to get into a good college/get a good job/get that first few promotions. They are so focused on these goals that they do not explore what it means to craft meaning for themselves in the world, so they either outsource that desire to institutions which award them for achieving these goals — thereby deriving their meaning from achieving relatively arbitrary goals with no definite end-point in sight — or they simply put this question off until they get that job/promotion/bachelor's degree.

Adulthood-as-crisis

By not exploring this imperative to create meaning when young, we force ourselves to put it off until later in life. This may be a fair tradeoff if it weren't for the fact that once we have set ourselves in economic, familial, and psychological ways, it is very hard to break loose of them. Entrepreneurship-oriented speakers oftentimes talk about how hard it is to go from a six-figure salary to $35,000/year as a startup founder and this holds true in the pursuit of meaning. If one finds later in life that they had not yet created meaning, it is hard to take a month off from work to try three different suspected "callings" before settling on one. It's hard to walk away from a family to pursue something different. It's hard to change later in life when we've given ourselves so much baggage.

Our conception of childhood-as-studentdom does not harm just the child but *also the adult into whom the child grows*. We deprive children of the opportunity to "just be kids," or to explore different aspects of life when the costs are low (i.e., no family, no major professional responsibilities, no rent to be paid, etc.).

Why are we doing this to ourselves and our children?

If the answer is "so they can at least be well-prepared for the realities of the world," then we have totally misaligned our priorities. Being "well-prepared for the realities of the world" is meaningless if it just means floating through life, just taking what is given to you, and not crafting meaning from it all. The goal ought to be to prepare people when they are young to know what they want, and *then* to go get it, not to go get some goal that brings a certain level of social approbation and hope that it coheres with what the individual wants.

So, Let's Abolish Childhood

We don't have to just accept this lot as the one which the universe gives us. We don't have to just tell ourselves, "oh well, I just hope that whatever goal I achieve when I grow up is one that brings me fulfillment." We can create a better system by which children can explore the world, live in it, not be sequestered away to a sterile environment for most days and can learn from their interactions in it. The hope is that this will help most children to discover what they do and do not want from life. They can learn first-hand what they need to know and what they need to strive towards.

This requires us to do away with the artificial division of life into childhood and adulthood. Children are simply persons growing into adults, and adults are simply persons who have grown past a certain point of biological development. They do not wield inherent authority over children that is not given to them in virtue of some other role (i.e., parent). Similarly, children are not something odd to be looked down upon and sequestered off. As soon as they exhibit an ability for sound judgement, they ought to be the primary decision-makers for those things in their lives over which they can exert agency. They ought to lead their own learning and exploration and only pull on adults when necessary for further instruction or for last-resort enforcement reasons in the rare case that children are naturally disagreeable.

The natural implication of this newfound respect for childhood and children is an abolition of the schools-as-we-know-them. Compulsory and standardized schooling is completely antithetical to the idea that children can learn when left to their own devices and are, in fact, just adults who spend the majority of their time learning and exploring the world.

Schools would not, as places of community and formal study, *need* to be done away with, but the standardized and compulsory nature of them must be. If we wish to allow children the very real freedom to explore their lives and take ownership over them — a freedom most adults do not fully explore until later in life — we cannot mandate they spend the majority of their time in some way learning subjects mandated by those removed from them.

...and Abolish Adulthood, Too.

If children are simply growing into adults, and adults are simply children who have passed a certain stage of development, then perhaps we ought not place such a seriousness on adulthood.

The consequence of immediately adopting this new perspective on childhood and adulthood would likely frighten many, but a generation of children raised with the respect and freedom owed to existentially-fulfilled adults would grow into a generation of adults much less fraught with anxiety and crisis about the world than those of recent generations.

The abolition of childhood may appear radical on the face, but is leaving an entire generation to the current system not *radically cruel* when we know we can do better?

HAYEK AND CAMUS WALK INTO A SCHOOL

There are practically as many philosophies of education as there are schools in the United States. There are the Prusso-American schools of Horace Mann's age, there are the public schools of the No Child Left Behind era, parochial schools of varying denominations, different types of military, boarding, and prep schools, Montessori, Waldorf, and Classical schools, and even major differences in philosophy of education for styles of homeschooling.

What, then, goes into a philosophy of education? What are the values and motivating thoughts behind questions like, "how are pupils to be educated?", "to what ends are they educated?", "who even are the pupils in this case?", "how is the school to be governed?"

Education ought to follow at least two points for providing young people with the freedom to craft meaningful lives for themselves:

- ☐ Practical understanding of problem-solving
- ☐ Freedom to craft individual meaning from the world

One of these points requires the acceptance of ignorance over the world while the other requires the acceptance of ownership. Pupils must take a skeptically aggressive creative stance towards their lives.

Practical Understanding of Problem-Solving

By "practical understanding of problem-solving," I don't mean that education should equip young people with abstract "problem-solving skills" that test designers and liberal arts professors always applaud as the goal of their respective programs. Rather, I mean to make a deeper point.

The world is complex and multifaceted and operates on a multitude of horizontal and vertical levels at once, with many moving parts and no real central design. Even designed systems have spontaneous orders developing in them, and are oftentimes the result of many systems that themselves come together to influence a planner beyond her own knowledge.

There's no surefire way to teach "problem-solving" because problems are themselves not centrally designed in the way that courses, exams, and assignments are. In fact, teaching young people that there are only one or two "right" and "wrong" answers to most questions and that those specific answers must be arrived at in a certain way (as many standardized tests do) only reinforces this mindset on them that problems are solved by following a formula.

Twelve years-straight of learning-to-the-test leads people to view the world in a different way than those who interact with its multifaceted nature on a daily basis. Add into that equation being at some form of school programs from 6 AM until 6 PM and then going home to do homework until 7 or 8 PM, and young people are forced to view the world in a very different, very structured way.

The world is not designed in the way of a classroom and *classrooms cannot be designed this way.* To create a classroom that has all the complexity and ever-moving parts of real world markets, norms, relationships, and informal institutions would require one to tear down the schoolhouse completely.

They become good at school and little else

FA Hayek wrote about the dangers of viewing the world as problems with cut-and-clear, centrally planned answers.

F.A. Hayek warned against this mindset, what he called "constructivism,"[1] in reference to constitutional design in his trio *Law, Legislation, and Liberty*. Hayek's commentary, while focusing on constitutional design and political order, can be applied to education. "Constructivism," or the belief that most or all institutions (including informal institutions like language, norms, mores, and mindsets) should or are "deliberately constructed by somebody," permeates the schooled mindset. Young people, who spend 12 or more years in an environment that is very much "deliberately constructed by somebody" have a difficult time adjusting to a world that has very little deliberate construction. Rather, the world is a series of overlapping and interdependent spontaneous orders, designed by no one person by reinforced, acted upon, and acting upon all who operate in the world.

While Hayek is arguing against central planners who believe they can design and control different aspects of the marketplace, the humility he preached is applicable to what young people ought to internalize in education. The world has problems to be solved, that much is true, but how to solve them, and by whom,

---

[1] I understand that the phrase constructivism means something entirely different in education theory. It actually means the exact opposite as Hayek means it in political economy. For the purposes of this section, the phrase constructivism refers to the Hayekian meaning of centrally designed order.

and in what ways are much more complex questions than traditional education gives justice to.

Freedom to craft individual meaning from the world

Being free to discover what gives one's own life meaning in the world is the most important aspect of living a fulfilled life. Becoming a successful, globally-renowned artist is an achievement for anybody, but it is only existentially fulfilling for some.

Traditional models of education have young people competing for the most prestigious/highest paying/most cushy college educations and jobs with the hope that they figure out what they find fulfilling along the way (this goes beyond schooling, and is actually a consequence of our mindset around childhood altogether).

This gets things backwards.

Young people aren't training to become successful adults if the "successful adults" they then grow into are footed with the bill asking them what it actually means to be successful.

Crafting meaning from the world should be the primary priority of any person, and the longer we force people to put this off and push it to the mental backburner — all while they get entrenched in schools, debt, careers, families, and more — the bigger injustice we do them.

Camus confronted this requirement to build meaning in his works.

In short, Camus says that life is devoid of inherent meaning. It is the job of every person to go out into the world and craft meaning for themselves from the host of options they have available. For some people, this may mean engaging in what others view as menial tasks. Camus goes as far as to say that we must even "imagine Sisyphus happy," as he rolls a boulder up a hill for eternity.

We can learn something from Camus' asburdism in the way we free childhood for crafting meaning. A successful life means different things for different people, but figuring out what that is should be the goal of education at any point in life. Once one formulates an idea of what success, greatness, or happiness means to them, they then go and acquire the skills and experience necessary to experience that (and these two things may happen simultaneously…it's just important that scarce time not be spent on acquiring skills and knowledge totally irrelevant to what the individual thinks will lead to fulfillment).

When young people spend thousands of hours over many years in a highly structured environment — and when this environment is further regulated to demand excellent test scores as the primary medium of success — it is no surprise that they find themselves with quarter-life crises asking what they really want to do with the decades ahead of them. Worse yet, they may find themselves with a mid-life crisis, wondering what they had just spent so many decades attempting to build.

Ignorance and Ownership

To extract the most value from a life-well-lived, we have to move away from the dominant education model which not only teaches young people that the world is a series of problems to be solved according to formulaic thought and action, but also deprives them of the ownership over creation of meaning in their lives and puts it off for years to come. Life is full of both ignorance over how complex the world works and ownership over the individual's sphere of influence.

Dominant forms of education do an injustice to young people, the adults they grow into, and their parents looking to raise them into fulfilled adults by depriving them of these two factors.

What we need is a system of freer education that allows people to see firsthand how complex the world is by tearing down the walls of the classroom and putting young people in the real world. They can take ownership over their lives without the permission of older people, and can start crafting this meaning early on.

We owe ourselves something better.

SOME WAYS TO THINK ABOUT SCHOOLING, PART I

Traditional schooling is unnatural, harmful, and stymies the social, intellectual, and cognitive development of young people. This is essentially the thesis of Boston College Psychologist Peter Gray's excellent 2013 work *Free to Learn*. Gray recounts his son telling him to "go to hell" after he and his wife try to keep him in a traditional school, where he is very clearly not meeting his fullest potential and acting out towards classmates and students. The book looks at anthropological and psychological work on the importance of play and the ways in which structured, top-down, administrator-to-teacher-to-student punitive schooling models[2] — like modern American public schools — fail to allow for the flourishing of these evolutionarily-imperative traits.

This is not a review of Gray's book but it raises an interesting point — how should we think of schooling?

---

[2] Throughout this post, I use the phrase "traditional schools" and variations on it. When I say that, I am referring to the classroom, teacher-in-the-front-with-administrators-over-her-shoulder model that American public schools embody. Most charter schools and private schools would also fall into this model.

Centralization And Individualism

Educational libertarians tend to support decentralization of education — the abolition of the Department of Education, returning power to local school boards, and allowing teachers and principals to make decisions appropriate for their students. But Gray's research would tell us that this doesn't go far enough (indeed, Gray says compulsory schools are by definition prisons). Most people who opt out of the traditional schooling model — whether they homeschool or use cyberschooling — don't do it primarily because of a federalism issue. They primarily do it for the issue of *freedom,* whether that is for their family or for the individual student.

So, we can think of common types of schooling on at least two verticals:

Centralized/Decentralized: How far removed are the deciders for curricular matters? Who gets to decide what the student, school, or curriculum looks like? Are they bureaucrats and politicians in the county seat? The state capital? Washington, D.C.? American public education is currently a heavily-centralized model, with some variation from state-to-state.

Collectivist/Individualist: Where does the learning take place? With how many people? Who gets to decide the pace of the learning? Traditional schools, where students sit in classrooms and the pace of the class is determined by an instructor, are collectivist rather than individualist. Cyber-schooling is moderately individualist and probably the most individualist form of centralized schooling since students can oftentimes engage with the content at their own pace, though the curriculum is set by somebody outside of the student's community (home, town, county).

If Gray and proponents of play-based models are correct, then a decentralized, individualist model like homeschooling would be superior to traditional schools.

	Decentralized	Centralized
Individualist	Homeschooling	Cyber-schooling
Collectivist	Local Traditional	Nationalized Traditional

Instructors And Community

Homeschooling and non-traditional schooling models come in their own unique flavors and variations. Go to any homeschooling convention and you can see this for yourself just by the titles of the breakout sessions and the exhibitors. The theme that ties all the attendees together is that they have the very strong belief that they can provide something better to their children than traditional schools. Once you get beneath that, you see there's an entire iceberg of variation.

Non-traditional schooling models can vary based on a number of different factors, but can be boiled down to at least two areas of major differences:

Instructor/No Instructor: Is there somebody who leads the learning? An adult in whom some kind of formal or informal authority is vested? This doesn't necessarily mean the adult has to impose a structured curriculum (i.e., "Today we will be studying X, Y, and Z. You have A, B, and C assignments,") but simply that they are recognized as the figureheads of a classroom.

Traditional homeschooling, while varying from family-to-family, will usually have a curriculum that a parent or instructor follows and requests the student to complete assignments.

Montessori Schools have trained instructors in them, who are akin to tools for the students to pull on while they are engaged in learning, they still ultimately control the structure of the day and can drive students towards one set of activities or another — they may lead them in song, art, or reading — but they *do not necessarily* impose a curriculum with assignments on the students.

Unschoolers go about their days and primarily learn from their interaction with the world around them. They may assign themselves work online, through books they have, or through real-world tasks, but they do not follow a formal curriculum.

Sudbury Schools are akin to unschooling insofar as there is not overarching structure to the year. There are no objective facts all students *must* learn. While adults are present, they are primarily there for legal purposes and to be used as tools for the students if the students wish for their help.

Personal/Communal: What's the environment like where students learn? Do they learn with other students, or will they largely (without additional tools or developments) be working with themselves and those very near to them?

	Instructor	No Instructor
Personal	Traditional Homeschools	Unschooling
Communal	Montessori Schools	Sudbury Schools

Traditional homeschooling and unschooling are primarily kept to the individual students, their families, and organizations or meet-ups the students and families may join.

Montessori Schools and Sudbury Schools are communal. The structure of the style of education has other young people built into it. Sudbury Schools are actually governed (i.e., administration) on a democratic basis, where students and adults get equal votes. This is why they are also known as "Democratic Schools."

We can break down the emphasis on curriculum even more. While Montessori and Traditional Homeschooling both have overarching objectives and goals, and while Sudbury and Montessori Schools are both communal, only Sudbury Schools have Open curricula and a Communal structure — leaving the goals and objectives learned by students to themselves to be determined (note of interest: this doesn't just mean that students do nothing for 12 years — they learn by interacting and playing with other students, asking older students to teach them skills, de-escalating situations with younger students, and eventually doing a graduation presentation to a panel at the end of the schooling — this is ultimately the style of education that Gray advocates in *Free to Learn).*

Open And Fixed Curriculum

Open/Fixed Curriculum: Are there objective goals to be achieved from the schooling? Is a curriculum used? Is success primarily measured on the basis of the ability of the student to meet the standards of the curriculum?

Traditional Homeschools often have fixed curricula — or curricula up to the discretion of the parent or instructor. They are akin to Traditional Schools in this sense.

Sudbury Schools and Unschooling provide the openness and freedom for students to experiment with the ends of their schooling and set those ends for themselves. The standards for success in these styles is much more subjective.

	Open	Fixed
Personal	Unschooling	Traditional Homeschooling
Communal	Sudbury Schools	Traditional Schools

Sudbury Schools can be thought of as **unschooling schools**. The characteristic that differentiates them from Montessori Schools is that Montessori education has an overarching structure and set of goals for students to achieve (and Montessori schools tend to only be pre-K-6 — Sudbury schools are the equivalent of pre-K-12), while this is left up to the student in Sudbury Schools.

Sudbury Schools prioritize the ability and development of the student to learn and educate themselves in a social environment and world. Practically, they provide an outlet for families that wish to unschool but can't for whatever reasons. Students learn what it is like to interact with people older and younger than themselves — they aren't divided into age-based classes like in Traditional Schools — and to solve the myriad social issues that come with that. They become life-learners, knowing how to learn from the child and adolescent's equivalent of "the real-world," because they are in it — something that Traditional School reformers (e.g., politicians, superintendents, consultants, principals, teachers) speak platitudes to, but rarely ever achieve.

Of course, there are more than just 5-7 types of schooling out there and other types can be organized by different manners. 2×2 matrices only allow us to think in terms of archetypes and extremes. Schooling styles exist on a spectrum and matrices can only do so much for us — but they allow us to organize the ways in which we think of different types of schooling and education.

SOME WAYS TO THINK ABOUT SCHOOLING, PART II: AUTHORITARIAN/LIBERTARIAN

In the last chapter, I offered a few different ways to think about and categorize different models of schooling and mapped some of these models onto 2×2 matrices. Schools can be categorized in terms of their curriculum (open/closed), their centralization (centralized/ decentralized), their setting of instruction (individualist/collectivist), and their setting of attendance (personal/communal).

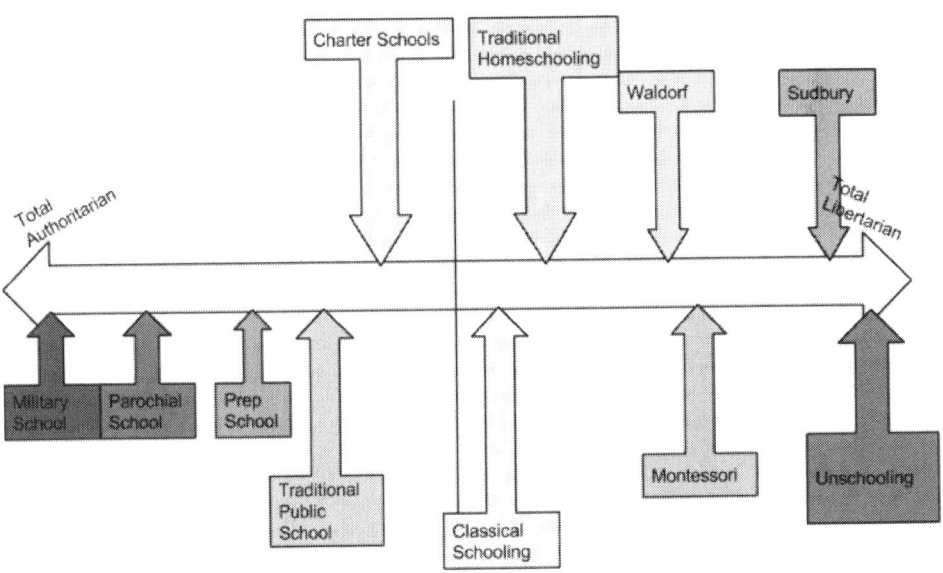

These allow us to categorize schools down different verticals and can be useful heuristics when comparing different types of schooling, but even these categories exist on a spectrum.

The most obvious spectrum in terms of schooling is one that is a composite of the above categories. I call this the **authoritarian/libertarian** spectrum, and it primarily reflects the pedagogical style, community, and ends of the schooling experience.

Authoritarian refers to the imposition of power and authority over the lives and curricula of students. A total authoritarian system not only controls the learning plans of students but also their lives through extracurricular activities, boarding mandates, and strict penal systems.

Libertarian refers to the lack of imposed power and authority on the student's life and curricula. A total libertarian system not only doesn't seep into and control the extracurricular components of a child's education, but also doesn't have any objective imposition of learning goals and objectives. Students set their curricula, what they want to learn, and how they will achieve it. Adults may be present to help them achieve these ends, but they aren't there to impose a specific set of things to be achieve on them.

On the **total authoritarian** end of the spectrum sits military schooling — which is designed to mirror military life, which itself is a hyper-hierarchical, authoritarian community. Orders are given by officers and followed by grunts, without any questions asked. Still in the authoritarian wing of the spectrum, but closer to the middle, sits traditional public schooling. Since traditional public schools are also organized on an order-and-command basis, and since they also strive towards the ends of creating good members for a community (the body politic), they still have a sense of authoritarianism about them. Some schools are less authoritarian than others, and some teachers are less than others, but the ends and general styles of the schooling technique are rooted in power, control, and authority.

On the **total libertarian** end of the spectrum sits unschooling. This type of schooling is so devoid of imposed power and authority that students create their own assignments and curricula. They design the structures of their days and their learning agendas. Sudbury schools sit close to total libertarianism, as students set the goals of their learning through play, and govern the structures of the schools through democratic vote. Adults are present but only to be pulled on as resources and for liability purposes.

Not included in the matrices yesterday was Waldorf Schooling — which is similar to Montessori schooling insofar as it is based off a specific style of pedagogy and includes broad, overarching goals for students to achieve. Waldorf schools are based off the educational insights of Rudolf Steiner, developed in 1919. Unlike Montessori schooling, Waldorf schools have instructors who *do* guide learning and curricular matters for students, so it falls further towards the authoritarian side of the spectrum than Montessori schools but is still quite libertarian, as the pedagogical style is itself is much more open than traditional schooling curricula.

To the surprise of some, traditional homeschooling sits towards the center of the spectrum, while still on the libertarian side. Just as the amount of imposed authority may change from public school-to-public school, the amount of imposed authority in the homeschool changes from family-to-family. Many homeschoolers are quick to point out that traditional homeschooling isn't unschooling. Indeed, go to any homeschooling convention and find that a good chunk of the exhibitors are companies devoted entirely to creating and selling homeschooling curricula and tools. Since homeschools don't *have to* have a strong sense of power and authority imposed on the student, they fall on the libertarian side of the spectrum in general.

Charter schools, while technically public schools, have more flexibility when it comes to the standardized requirements imposed by regulators, so students may have more flexibility to explore their ends within the classroom.

It may strike some as odd to use the words "authoritarian" and "libertarian" to refer to schooling. "Schooling is just a fact of life, to use the same word to describe schools as one would use to describe a dictatorship is hyperbole." Authoritarian schools — military schools, compulsory public schools, traditional parochial schools — may not be dictatorships, but they are strikingly similar to prison — another authoritarian system. In prisons people have no choice as to whether they are there or not, and their actions throughout the day are tightly controlled and regulated. In traditional schools, students are moved from class-to-class at a bell's notice, their behavior is closely monitored and regulated, and they have no choice as to whether or not they can leave.

Schooling may be "a fact of life," but that doesn't mean that it has to mirror an outdated form of 19th century German military schooling. Unschooling, Montessori, Sudbury, Homeschooling, and Waldorf schools show us that there are options outside of the paradigm many of us grew up in.

A BRIEF DEFENSE OF PLAYING-AS-LEARNING

An indignant commenter on one of the pages I follow argues with homeschool parents on Facebook, saying they only opposed public schools because they did poorly in them and they are bad facilitators of learning because they let their children play.

This commenter is a former teacher herself, and lauds her institution-backed expertise in the field of mathematics as making her qualified to speak on the matter. What she misses is that the parents who let their children play *are* excellent facilitators. By giving their children the freedom to engage in meaningful behavior, as simple as playing outside, they are giving them the opportunity to really, truly, learn.

Why is this? What does freedom have to do with true, valuable learning?

To parse this out, we have to work backwards with the status quo of compulsory schooling.

If we assume that human beings are naturally curious creatures then it makes sense that their natural state is one predispositioned towards learning and engaging deeply in the world around them. They have an implicit expectation that this is how discovering the world around them takes place. Watch a baby play with a remote control, a toy car, or just a piece of paper. They smack it around, chew on it, throw it, and eventually figure out how it is "supposed" to work and have a great time while doing so. They don't see learning and playing as two separate things.

As they grow older into the world, they are naturally driven towards this mindset. Children playing with legos discover how things fit together, how buildings must be built for basic structural integrity, and how to interact with other children. *Minecraft,* a favorite of young children, allows them to build things, tear them down, and put them back together again. They learn the difference between wood, rock, dirt, and more. They learn the value of work to extract wood. They may play *SimCity* and learn basic city planning and the economics related to it.

Then comes along a forced instructor. This may be an overzealous parent, a schoolteacher, or a priest. This person tells the child (now relegated to the status of "student") that they *must* engage in certain activities and learn certain things. The path towards which they were naturally driven has now been blocked and their mental energy siphoned elsewhere. Unless they are lucky and the starting-grounds for instruction just happen to align with what their interests are at that time, they resent instruction. Over time, they come to associate instruction with schooling, schooling with "learning," (since advocates of compulsory schooling have co-opted the word and made it synonymous in popular vernacular with schooling), and they associate learning with the resentment they felt at being told to learn long division.

Resentment has a long history with varied analysis, going at least back to Bishop Joseph Butler's Sermons at Rolls Chapel. At its core, it is the frustration of expectations. John has expectation A for his day, but Janine inserts herself into his life by no choosing of John's own and determines his day will revolve around Janine's expectation B. John resents this frustration of his expectations. The phrase "expectations" is a catchall that can be used to describe formal expectations — like those of a contract or a vow — or informal expectations — like norms and mores.

Even young children can have "expectations." These are the subconscious strata on which they operate. At the most basic level, these can be anthropologically explained as "the natural way" people learn. So, when somebody else comes into a situation and says "you *must* learn what I say," they frustrate the expectations of the child and create resentment.

Freedom is the cure to this resentment of learning. Sure, learning by playing outside may not *look* like schooling, but it is much more in line with how young humans have come to learn over time. By not imposing what must be learned, and therefore not frustrating the expectations of the young, we allow them to flourish in their relationship with learning (or at least come to repair it after damage done by well-meaning educators and not-so-well-meaning planners).

Boston College psychologist Peter Gray summarizes playing-as-learning with this sonnet posted at his blog; it is a good way to think lightly on the subject:

"In play we learn to think in ways most clear.
In play with others we resolve our strife.
In play we laugh at what provokes our fear.
In play we soar above our routine life.
In play we learn to follow rules we share,
Assert our selves while making others smile.
In play what's right is what to all is fair.
In play it's fun to go the extra mile.
And so to you the god of play we pray,

Please keep our ludic spirit's liveliness.
As we approach the trials of each day,
Protect us from our over-seriousness.
From dust to dust we all end up the same.
*What counts in life is how we play the game."*ˣ

Refer to Further Reading for more information on Gray's work.

IN PRAISE OF LAISSEZ-FAIRE TEACHERS

I was publicly schooled all through my upbringing (minus a Montessori pre-K that I attended) and I am — by all conventional measures — fairly successful so far in life. I can read, write, and do calculations on the right-side of a normal distribution, I was accepted to an Ivy League institution, I've worked on a growing startup, and I've written and spoken publicly. "Why then," it is sometimes asked, "are you so opposed to the schooling that did so well for you?"

I don't oppose traditional public schooling because it is public, but because of its standardization. And I don't oppose the standardization because of the content of it (ala many opponents of Common Core), but because standardization across the education spectrum teaches children to relegate their independent thought and faculties to things outside of "thinking," and to conceive of thinking as work to be done under threat of force.

I was *fortunate* for much of my time in my school because I had excellent teachers. I had teachers who were quite talented at teaching and knew their subjects well — but they aren't the excellent teachers I am thinking of here. I am thinking of the teachers who left me and my classmates to our own devices. I am thinking of the teachers who used their classrooms as safe-havens of self-directed learning and bastions of experimentation in thought. I am thinking of the teacher who, if somebody merely glanced into the classroom, would think they spent most of their time at the desk, not "teaching," but in reality are leading the best opportunity for children and young adults to learn and to teach others.

I am thinking of the laissez-faire (hands-off) teachers. These teachers allowed me to have a reprieve from the drill of instruction throughout the day and a place to go where I could flourish into a young adult who could think critically of the world around him (not to say that I think I turned out perfect...).

These teachers are vindicated as their students grow older and have greater depth in their interests and their conceptions of the happy life.

I could always respond to the "well you didn't turn out so bad," criticism by saying I can't play counterfactuals — because I can't — but I find this more useful. I didn't turn out so bad *in spite of* standardization. Those teachers who allowed for free expression, exploration, and development of thought are the true schoolteachers of the public administration.

HOW "BELOW AVERAGE" KILLS DREAMS

When I was in school, once or twice a year my family would receive an official report from the school district telling them about my performance on various metrics. I was reading at an advanced level, doing math at an above-average level, my PSSA scores were high, and so on.

At first, these reports made me happy and excited. This meant my work was being reflected in something that could be measured and, more importantly, meant that I wouldn't have a school bureaucrat breathing down my neck every spring before exams. Over time, I realized something insidious about them, brought on by the disparity between my math and reading scores.

My math scores were still above average, but they were lower than my reading scores, and always had been since I could do elementary math. How could this be? I could read at a collegiate level and do formal logic, but I couldn't learn math as well? I could do calculus, advanced statistics, physics, and chemistry, but a standardized test told me I could still improve on its standards.

Consider the ways in which I learned the fundamentals of each:

Reading — While my parents read to me when I was little and I engaged in language-related activities when young, I remember spending day-in-and-day-out playing video games in my free time on my family's old Apple computer. Some of these games were primarily operated via images — drag-and-drop, painting games, picture games — but some used text. They didn't use high-level text, but made use of text in the story and throughout the plot to move the game along. Many could be played without making the text out, but reading would make it much easier and enjoyable. Over time, I simply picked up how to read from increasingly-complex video games (and later, books).

Math — While I did do some math in video games and could learn addition and subtraction by it easily, most of my introduction to math came in school and at times when I would have rather been learning about taxonomies or geography. Once division was introduced — and the increasingly convoluted ways of teaching it that schoolteachers like to use — I was largely lost. I came to view math, something once seen in video games as a fun challenge, as work. I didn't want to do it and it was the bane of my evenings.

In time, I ended up enjoying math, but only through the freedom to use it in clubs and extracurricular events (e.g., music activities, physics activities, statistics, etc.) from which I derived meaning. While reading and writing came naturally to me and were the bedrocks of the things I enjoyed doing, math was different. It would have come to me in time naturally, but was forced earlier than I had wanted to learn it.

Juxtapose this further with logic. Formal and symbolic logic *look* like math. There are equations and problem sets and logic is ultimately the foundation of math. I have and had no problem learning logic. I picked it up as a side-project my senior year of high school and have enjoyed it since.

How could this be? How could I engage with two strikingly similar fields in very different ways?

Consider the following quotation from Ivan Illich's *Deschooling Society*:

> *Most learning is not the result of instruction. It is rather the result of unhampered participation in a meaningful setting. Most people learn best by being "with it," yet school makes them identify their personal, cognitive growth with elaborate planning and manipulation.*

When learning reading or logic or geography or history or civics or science — anything *not based on long division* — I found ways to incorporate it into games or pretend stories I would draw up in my mind or in video games. Even logic was something I did because I thought philosophy was interesting and I wanted to learn more about it.

Math, meanwhile, was taught as, "first you need addition, then you need subtraction, then you need multiplication, and now division...and now long division," (with a math teacher of mine even playing up the difficulty of long division for elementary schoolers). Problems could only be solved and given points if you "showed your work" and did the work in the way the teacher wanted. Even if you arrived at the correct answer through your own devices or through "mental math," points were deducted because it "isn't the right way."

It is no wonder that young me and so many young children like myself grew to resent math. We were denied the opportunity and time to engage with it in a meaningful setting where we could "be with it," and were forced to learn it in the way specified for arbitrary reasons.

(Aside: this is why complaints about the ridiculous ways in which Common Core-based textbooks teach math should be taken seriously. When children are taught that problems can only be solved correctly in abstruse ways with counter-intuitive reasoning, they'll likely internalize that their own ways of naturally solving them are wrong and that they are wrong for having them.)

And I'm not alone. Consider at the other end of the spectrum, the Sudbury Valley School in Framingham, MA doesn't tell students, "Maybe you should learn X," because that pressures them into an environment where they don't derive their own meaning as readily from the experience of learning.

Some students at the school start reading at age 6, some at 7, some at 8, some at 9, and some even at 11. By age 15, all the students read at the same level and are no worse off for it. The girl who didn't read until age 11 may come to love reading and may make a career out of working in writing. While others were reading ahead of her by age, she wasn't pressured into feeling bad or wrong for not doing the same.

In traditional, standardized schools, the illiterate 10 year old would be put in remedial classes, kept away from peers, and told that she has to go to "special education" classes because she doesn't read at a level the teachers and bureaucrats have chosen is right for her age. It is likely that she'll come to resent reading, and will forever lag behind other students in it. She'll read books and view each sentence as work to be overcome, not an engagement that flows effortlessly from the first to the second and onward. Even though she would have likely been fine if simply left to her own devices, the school sets her up for self-doubt, shame, and potential failure.

This may be an extreme case, but even telling or nudging a young person, still feeling their way and passions about the world, "Maybe you should spend more time on X," or "Why don't you learn Y?" or "It would be so fun to learn Z! Don't you think?" sets them up for self-doubt if their response, after learning it, is "Maybe I shouldn't have learned X," or "Z isn't that much fun, what must be wrong with me?"

A better solution is to let go of the anxiety of being "below average." "Below average" at 11 means nothing unless compared to what happens at age 15, 17, 25, 35, and onward. Telling a child she is "below average" or even "below expectations for her age," doesn't inspire her to work harder — it makes her question her relationship to the schooling at hand and associate that question with true, real, valuable learning.

The fact of the matter is that different people learn things at different times and in different ways. By attaching "right" to when most people decide to learn something (or force themselves to do it because of schooling), we label those who do it other ways that they are "wrong," and start to close the doors for them to "learn by being 'with it.'"

YOUR HIGH SCHOOL FRIENDSHIPS DIED OUT? REJOICE!

I recently had an opportunity to meet up with a friend of mine from high school. He actually went to a different school, but we shared similar values and traveled in similar extracurricular circles, so we stayed in touch over the years after graduating. We chatted over what we had accomplished in the preceding years, where we were thinking of going in life, and reminisced a little about people we knew.

We both found ourselves saying that several of our friendships that we thought at the time would last us a lifetime — or at least until we turned 30! — ended up fizzling out pretty quickly after high school. Save a meetup here on a break from school or a Facebook message there, the friendships we had spent years of our relatively young lives building had fallen by the wayside.

Some — perhaps most — people would be tempted to get romantic here and try to rekindle these friendships. Many have made such attempts — I did on multiple occasions. These were usually just to friends telling me they only thought of speaking with me when drunk or when thinking about some weird, niche subject only I was interested in learning more about.

There's a sentimental tug when you go back to your hometown or see on Facebook that a friend from high school is nearby. You may even exchange messages about "reconnecting" or "grabbing coffee," but rarely does anything come to fruition. You slowly come to realize that you probably aren't going to really reconnect with this person again — save for obligatory functions like a potential funeral or outing in the same city.

Your friendships with people from high school die out. Later in life, a good chunk of your friendships from college will follow the same path. This may seem like a tragedy — you'll have your memories that you wish you could relive — but it really isn't. It's to be expected.

Most formal schooling is not chosen by the student. The setting, the atmosphere, the subjects, and the classmates are all left more or less up to chance. The chance of your parents living in one ZIP code or another, the chance of your last name starting with one letter or another, and the chance of you being born on one date rather than another.

You go about your years in grade school sorted with people who fall into similar ranges of ZIP code and age. You divide further based on your last name and a few characteristics that are more or less arbitrary — like your ability to read at age 5 or your ability to play sports. You may develop real, sincere interests in the years that follow, but you are still stuck around these same groups of people.

As you age, you may be allowed to "elect" to attend certain classes that reflect your interests. Band, shop, art, or a language class are now open to you. Chances are you'll bond better with the students in those classes than in your mathematics or your English classes. All that being said, you still *do* build bonds with people. You find a few friends in the rough. Through all the hormones and the tumultuousness of puberty and public schooling, you find some comrades who hang in there along with you while you all try your hardest to get out.

But here's the thing about the vast majority of the relationships that you build in school: **they're entirely artificial.** These are not real, natural friends because school is not a real, natural environment. (I mean "real" and "natural" in the sense that it evolves from the free choices of free beings — not in a 'don't harm Mother Earth' sense.)

Real, natural friendships are formed based on shared values, mutual interests, and a common respect for a vision of the community you wish to build in your life. When your choices for community are so limited and controlled as they are in school, your options for friendship become limited and distorted.

If you were afforded the freedom and the flexibility of normal human beings during your formative years, you likely would have never associated with these people or even had the chance to associate with them. With the exception of the select few with whom you are friends because of their values, most of these people are friends out of necessity. The pickings are slim, and when they are, you get what you can take.

This isn't to say that all high school-aged people are sociopaths calculating their way to the top — rather, this happens in good nature. These people are the closest thing to real, natural friends in the fake, unnatural environment that is school.

Once you get to college, you get a little more freedom and flexibility to choose your friends. Then, you hit the "real" world and you have total freedom relative to your earlier years. You can associate with whom you want. You can spend time with whom you want. You can cut people out of your life at will. Don't like your coworkers? Quit your job. Don't like the people in your town? Move. Don't like your "friends"? Find new friends. The freedom is magnitudes greater than that afforded to a child or a young adult.

Your friendships from high school are dying or dead? College, too?

Rejoice!

You now have the opportunity to build real, lasting friendships based on shared values, mutual beliefs, and fostering a community based on your interests. Take this opportunity and run with it. Build the life that you want — the one that reflects your values.

Section 2: The Reality of School

Most learning is not the result of instruction. It is rather the result of unhampered participation in a meaningful setting. Most people learn best by being "with it," yet school makes them identify their personal, cognitive growth with elaborate planning and manipulation.

Ivan Illich

THE GREATEST LIE WE TELL CHILDREN

One of the greatest lies we tell young children is that they go to school to learn.

At one point or another, the absurdity of compulsory schooling strikes most young children — not yet jaded by years of routine and dulling expectations — and they ultimately ask a parent, teacher, mentor, or older person, "why do I *have* to go to school?" Usually, the response goes along the lines of, "You have to go to school so that you can learn." As children get older and become young adults, the explanation goes from kindly information to borderline coercive, "You have to go to school so you aren't flipping burgers your whole life!" Something happens in these years that the focus — at least in what we tell children the point of school is — goes from knowledge to professional signaling.

There's a real danger to telling young children that they *must* go to school so that they must learn. The exploitation of this danger is of paramount importance to inculcating a schooled mindset. It essentially goes like this:

"You must go to school so you can learn!" implies that *not* going to school means the child will not learn. Children, naturally both curious of the world around them and trustworthy of adults, take this information to mean that, should they want to embrace the world around them and engage with it at a deeper level, they have to go to school in order to do that.

Only that that isn't what happens. After several years of monotonous exercises, following schooling regimen to the letter, and associating learning with schooling, and schooling with the natural authoritarianism of the schooled setting, children start to resent *learning itself.*

This resentment only grows with age. As young adults, we begin to form our life-plans for ourselves and set ourselves on the path to what we want from our lives. Compulsory school becomes more than just an authoritarian day camp — it becomes an immediate burden to our ability to live our happy lives. It not only burdens us by taking up the time and energy from our lives, but also deepens our resentment of anything that may formally be called "learning."

This is the greatest lie because learning is at the core of our lives as human beings. We *must* learn to survive. We evolved a strong system to learn quickly and intuitively —play. But schools are the exact opposite of play. Play is spontaneously structured — or structured around rules that have developed over time — voluntary, and fun. School is centrally planned, coercive, and — for the vast majority of students — miserable. While humans are meant to associate learning with play (and therefore, the voluntary fun it brings with it), compulsory schooling replaces play with school and the dread it brings with it. It thereby stunts the individual's ability to engage in learning as easily, and limits their ability to live out their life to the potential they may aspire to.

The coopting of the language of education by advocates of compulsory schooling in the 20th century was the greatest crime to learning committed in recent history. It was also the best thing that could possibly have been done for such advocates, as well-intending parents and educators now could not oppose their reforms, lest they be opponents of "learning," too.

The first path to regaining control over education and learning is taking control of the language. If you are deschooling yourself, *never* let somebody tell you you're not learning. Never let them get away with "how are you learning, then?" Rather, ask them, "You mean to tell me you spend 9 hours every day in the same building? Doing things other people make you? How do you learn, then?" Take control over the language just as you take control over your own education.

THERE NEVER WAS A GOLDEN AGE OF HIGHER ED

The popular notion that there was a golden age of higher education tends to argue that higher education *once* was a place where young people came to have their minds opened by erudite academics, gain the skills and work ethic necessary to succeed in the workplace, and develop into the mature, successful young adults ready to take on the world — all at a fair price. This was a time when higher education was a place that prepared young people for the world ahead of them. This was a time when getting more young people to attend college is one of the best things a society could do — it could invest in its future.

This notion is decidedly wrong.

There never was a golden age of higher education. There never was a time when college was the best place to prepare young people for the lives ahead of them. There never was a time when it was the best option for a young person to go to college for four years immediately after high school, study, and then go into the workplace.

This time didn't exist fifty years ago and it certainly does not exist today when access to educational capital sits in the pocket of every person in a modernized country through their smartphones and high-tech laboratory equipment sits in startups and multinational corporations alike.

A Place For Bureaucrats

College is an institution that is good at creating highly-specialized experts in a select few areas, all of which have academic cartels in common as their central means of employment: professors, doctors, lawyers, and bureaucrats.

Beyond these highly-specialized savants, spending four years in college is one of the worst things an ambitious young person can do. Not only do they subject themselves to an institution that was decidedly *not* built for their goals and is run by people decidedly *not* in their aspiring fields, they do so at the cost of not being entrenched in the marketplace.

Diving into the marketplace and learning and applying a skill set there carries a variety of strong advantages over studying in academia and then attempting to carry over skills to the marketplace.

Better Options In The Marketplace

The market is a multifaceted system of positive- and negative-feedback loops. Through a price system of profit and loss, firms can get a better idea of what works and doesn't work than by going to a central authority whose expertise is to be trusted on the matter (as in academia). Further, individuals in firms can get a better idea of what tactics, skills, and strategies work better for them within the firm by working with a small team whose projects make an impact on the profit-direction of the firm. In this way, the marketplace is a more robust short-term adaptation mechanism to guide individuals for what they need to learn and better in their day-to-day habits and training.

The market as a whole responds more quickly to technological innovation and cultural evolution than academia does. By not only being the primary benefactor of new technology — but often the mother of new tech — marketplace firms have a strong incentive to hire for and train their employees in the most efficient and effective technology and skills needed to produce value.

I was recently speaking to a young coder and designer who wanted to learn a highly specialized skill set for a program he is working on. He was too young to enroll in collegiate courses on the topic but didn't seem to care. He found the information available online, skipped the superfluous prerequisite courses, and gleaned the skills necessary to feel confident in launching his project. I asked him why he didn't just go audit courses at a local (acclaimed) university.

"Why would I? They would be years behind where the companies working on this tech are right now."

In an academic setting, he would have been told that he must take the prerequisite courses before he could study what he wanted to use for his project — and then likely wouldn't have gleaned the necessary information given the outdated and slow-moving nature of academia.

This isn't a blunt insult against academia or a bias, either. It makes sense when you look at the incentives that professors have.

Incentives Matter

A tenured professor of computer science doesn't have much incentive to update and improve his courses for his students. At best, it's his conscience that guides him and tells him he shouldn't be teaching incoming freshmen something that he knows is 10 years outdated. Maybe some advisors of some sort urge him to update his class.

This takes work, though, and he likely has a research agenda that helps him stay well-fed and funded. Updating the syllabus to stay up-to-date with technological developments would take hours of work, research, and putting together new assignments.

It gets pushed to the backburner. He'll take care of it when he has time, he says. He probably has a GA revise it in a few years (who, himself, has incentive to turn his attention elsewhere).

A company, on the other hand, has every incentive possible to stay up-to-date on new tech. Entire departments are hired just with the goal of training employees on new developments. Firms undertake espionage missions against each other to figure out what their competitors are using and developing. They hire for candidates with the most up-to-date knowledge of the relevant technology and skills.

Failure to do so leads to failure of the employees to build the best product possible for consumers. Failing to build the best product possible is a recipe for disaster.

If you want to learn new skills that are highly relevant and will be the best for you to add value to society, go to the marketplace, not academia.

And this has always been the case.

Just because Penn had the laboratories that were able to build some of the first computers doesn't mean it was the best place to learn how to use computers. IBM had more incentive to train employees in the relevant tech than Penn did to train students.

Incentives Matter For Students, Too

Think of the incentives that act upon students in K-12 and then in college. What do they get disapprobation for? What do they get approbation for? How is the institution structured with which incentives for young people?

A typical student is going to focus on what the person with immediate and direct control over their quality of life in a given context wants. In classes, this is the instructor. Students will focus on what they believe will make the instructor give them a high mark rather than what they believe is the best quality of their work or what is the best approach they can take. Sometimes, instructors succeed and provide students with the right incentives to turn in assignments that would be acceptable in the marketplace (for which the students are supposedly being prepared).

This is rarely the case.

We shouldn't expect students, then, to put in inordinate time outside of class to learn what the market wants — they have little immediate incentive to do so while enrolled as students.

If they were to throw off the shackles of academia and jump into creating value for others, they would have to follow a different beat. The immediate incentive is set by what their client wants. They have incentive to figure out how to best create value for other people — if they fail to do so, they feel the pain of loss/if they succeed in doing so, they feel the reward of profit.

Incentives matter for both professors and students. The best incentive for self-betterment and skill development comes outside academia entirely.

Don't Lie To Young People

There's never been a golden age of higher education for a young person who doesn't want to be a professor, doctor, lawyer, or bureaucrat. The incentives have always been this way. Trying to tell young people there was or is dangerous for them and for the quality of the value they can add to society in the future.

HOW SCHOOLS LIMIT OUR LIVES WITH PERMISSION

May I go to the bathroom?

May I borrow a pencil?

May I have next Monday off to go on a family vacation?

These questions and ones like them are going to be asked countless times today and over the course of the next couple of months. Everybody from first graders to adult high school seniors and even their parents will ask for things like whether or not it is acceptable for them to use the bathroom, whether or not they can take their children with them on a family retreat, and whether or not they can borrow a pencil.

This is a central feature of the schooled mindset — students are forced to ask for permission for anything as little as enforcing basic bodily functions before they can rightly act upon them. Enforced under the guise of cordiality and good manners, schools' permission requirements teach young people that there will be an authority from which they must seek permission before they can do anything — and they carry this mindset with them through life.

Even in college, young adults still seek permission from professors to go to the bathroom, request days off for basic family functions, and see themselves as subject to the authority of the classroom despite being grown adults. It expands beyond petty classroom requirements to careers, too. Graduates expect that they can't go into business if they graduate with a liberal arts degree and need feel-good articles showing others who have done it successfully before they'll consider it. They think that if they haven't taken a class on economics, then they probably shouldn't try to read more on the subject (although they're happy to have opinions on the subject come election time). It bleeds into their parenting styles and they are raised by and/or become helicopter parents and believe their children must ask them for permission on careers and basic lifestyle choices before they can act on them. They think they have to have some sort of approval from *somebody* before they can pursue their careers — this can be the university, a college recruiter, a book about what they can do with their degree, their parents, it doesn't matter — they've fallen into the trap of a permission-based mindset.

And it's not entirely their faults. They go through 12-16 years of what is essentially a constructed mini-society. When you spend 5 out of 7 days a week in a controlled environment with clear authorities, clear structures, and clear ways to "win" and "lose," you will probably start to view the world that way. If you spend all these years in a system where your actions are entirely dependent on the approval or disapproval of one or several individuals never more than a few levels removed from you, you'll probably view yourself as subject to these decisions and permission of people not too far from you for much of your young life.

This is one of the features of a **constructivist** order. Constructivism is, as put by FA Hayek, a belief that an order or system was purposefully designed by people and that it can be understood in this context. There are planners and designers and boards and commissars who decide what goes where for which use when. A command-control economy is a good example of a constructivist view of the world. This is to be contrasted with a **spontaneous order**, or a order or system that is emergent from the decisions and actions of many people. An example of a spontaneous order is a free market economy that is able to allocate resources to build a pencil — an amazingly complex task.

Schools are miniature examples of constructivism. There's no sense of an economy in a school — all resources are managed and directed by different advisors, managers, and administrators. The rules that govern the school are laid out very clearly in a student handbook — and although norms and mores may arise in the hallways and on the playgrounds, they're unplanned — and a board governs appoints an administrator to govern how teachers spend their time with students. Students are always subject to another direct authority, either a teacher, vice principal, principal, guidance counselor, superintendent, school board member, or a bureaucrat off in the state capitol.

In a constructivist society, it's the same way. You must have permission from the foreman, or the local commissar, or the state commissar, or the planner in Moscow. Your actions are determined by a schedule that you have very little control over and what you have options in is entirely determined by the options you had previously.

"Well, that just sounds like life, what's wrong with that?"

After several generations are thoroughly schooled, this permission-based mindset becomes rampant throughout a culture. It's so rampant in modern American society — where nearly everybody goes through some form of compulsory schooling — that it doesn't strike us as odd anymore. It should, especially if we still believe that individuals are individuals and that no one person or group of people is more fit to rule or to organize society than any other. Whether we believe in the efficient ways of spontaneous orders on a societal level or in the moral equivalence of all individuals, the idea that any one group is better fit to rule you or your life should be incredibly foreign.

On a personal level, if you have ever envisioned yourself doing something that doesn't require the permission of other people to achieve, then you should reject the permission-based mindset. If you've ever thought about creating a 4-hour workweek, launching your own business, or becoming an artist, you **must** reject this mindset. There will be other people out there who tell you that you can't do those things; "you aren't playing by the rules," "what about your career?" "How can you do that if you don't have a business/art degree?" They will start to wear down on you if you don't reject this mindset entirely.

For many people, this permission-based mindset won't seem like anything odd. It will just seem like the way things are. You go to school, score good test scores, attend the best college you are allowed to for your dollar, and then either go off to become a doctor/lawyer/consultant if you're lucky. If you're less ambitious, you'll go do your 9-5 that you ask permission for once you graduate and can live your life on the side so long as you have the permission to do so.

If either of those truly calls out to you, then don't see that as a slight. For some people, becoming a doctor, lawyer, or consultant is what they really want to do. For others, though, it's an expectation. Once you reach the end of the permission-oriented system that is K-12, the obvious continuation is more permission-oriented systems like pre-med/pre-law/business school, and then graduate school, and then a job that very much mirrors that K-12 system.

If that doesn't call out to you, realize that you don't need anybody's permission to live your life, just like the 8 year-old who doesn't need anybody's permission to go to the bathroom.

SCHOOL IS CREATING A GENERATION OF UNHAPPY PEOPLE

It's said that pain isn't the opposite of happiness — boredom is.

With this premise in mind, is it any surprise that children, adolescents, and young adults today are so unhappy?[xi] Is it any surprise that so many turn to extending their schooled lives into structured activities as long as possible? Is it any surprise that when people don't know what to do, they simply go to graduate school?

To understand this mass unhappiness and boredom with life — and the sudden uptick in quarter-life crises — look at where these young people have spent most of their lives.

What we see today in Millennials and younger is something henceforth unseen in the United States: a fully-schooled generation. Every young person, save the occasional homeschooler, today has been through schools. This means rich & poor, established & unestablished, and developed & undeveloped young adults have all been put through roughly the same exact system with the same general experiences for the last two decades of their lives.

School teaches them that life is broken into discernible chunks and that learning and personal development are to be seen as work. Rather than teaching them how to foster a love of learning, a constantly-centralizing school regime in the US today teaches them to look for standards to be measured against. Rather than helping give them the cognitive and philosophical tools necessary to lead fulfilled lives in the context of the world in which they live, schools remove them from this world and force them to develop these skills only after 18-25 years of being alive. Rather than allowing them to integrate themselves into the broader scheme of life and learn what they get fulfillment from achieving and what they don't, school leaves fulfillment to five letter grades and a few minutes of recess.

> *"We destroy the love of learning in children, which is so strong when they are small, by encouraging and compelling them to work for petty and contemptible rewards, gold stars, or papers marked 100 and tacked to the wall, or A's on report cards, or honor rolls, or dean's lists, or Phi Beta Kappa keys, in short, for the ignoble satisfaction of feeling that they are better than someone else." — John Holt*

In short, school teaches apathy towards education and detachment from the world. School removes people from being forced to learn how to get fulfillment from a variety of activities and subjects and instead foists a handful of clunky subjects onto them hoping they meet state standards for "reading," "mathematics," "writing," and "science."

Not only this, but they've had childhood extended further into adulthood than any other generation before them. A young person today is considered a "child" much longer than a young person 20 or 40 years ago would have been considered as much. To treat a 16 year-old as a child in the 1960s would have been insulting. Today, it is commonplace.

Adult children wander the hallways of universities and workplaces today, less-equipped to find purpose and meaning than their predecessors. They can't be entirely blamed for their anxiety and depression — their parents, teachers, and leaders put them through an institution and created a cultural norm that created the world they live in today.

This is the perfect formula for creating a group of constantly bored people. They've been deprived of a chance to find meaning for themselves in subjects by engaging with them on a deep level and internalizing the responsibility necessary to live in the world. They've been cut off from opportunities to make real connections with people based on more than a lottery of ZIP codes for a decade. They've been taught that achievement is getting to the next level set by people outside of themselves.

Pain isn't the opposite of happiness — boredom is. A fully schooled generation has created a generation of bored adult children. It's no wonder young people today seem so unhappy.

SOME BAD ARGUMENTS AGAINST HOMESCHOOLING

If you pull the average American off the street and ask them to describe what they think the average homeschool family looks like, they'd probably paint the picture of a bunch of children and adults wearing pleated khakis, button-downs with sweaters, and who are socially awkward, sheltered and overly-structured in their lives (or, oddly enough, totally unstructured in their lives and constantly causing chaos).

In Europe, homeschoolers face even more scrutiny. Seen as cultists by the media at large, they are treated even worse than domestic terrorists in some central and western European nations.

Even people who are more libertarian in terms of education would likely say, "sure, I don't think it should be illegal, but *I'd* never do it myself. ... How would the children become socialized? ... I wouldn't want to spend that much time around my children. ..."

The arguments against homeschooling are many and the vast majority of them are bad. While homeschooling — which I define here in the legal sense of simply meaning not sending children to a school, so this includes traditional homeschooling and unschooling — isn't necessarily for everybody, the popular arguments against it are lazy and easily disproven.

There's a constant theme through many of these arguments — they're lazy because they are almost always only applied to homeschoolers. The people who ask them rarely ask them of the obvious alternatives — traditional schools (particularly traditional public schools) — and argue against homeschooling with the intention to say that putting children in a traditional school would be better. This *status quo bias* is a tricky psychological situation for most people to break out of. They come to see what is most common around them as "normal," "natural," and "good," without seriously questioning it. If many of the arguments below were applied to traditional schools, the schools would collapse tomorrow from parents withdrawing their children in outrage.

While rebuttals are easy and obvious once you actually interact with homeschoolers and see that they are rarely the stereotype people imagine, the best way to get people to see past their preconceived notions is to meet them in the real world. Change happens by people not realizing it is happening. Social norms and attitudes towards same-sex relationships, for example, were largely changed by people meeting same-sex couples and seeing that they are by and large normal people. Arguments are only so good — get out there and meet detractors in the real world.

"How will your child learn X?" or **"How are you qualified to teach Y?"**

This is one of the most common and intuitive objections to homeschooling. In the politicized, ideal version of traditional schools, teachers are experts who are not only well-versed in their fields, but also well-versed in pedagogy. Removing children from this environment implies that they will be receiving training and instruction from somebody equally as qualified in, say, mathematics.

Even if the idealized version of traditional schools was accurate, this doesn't mean that parents have to have a teaching certificate in mathematics for the child to learn math. Homeschoolers often have curricula designed by people trained in these fields, can hire tutors, or can turn to technology to learn what they need to help their children learn.

"Okay, fair for traditional homeschooling, but what about for unschoolers? If you don't have a curriculum, how do you expect the child to learn Z?"

While unschooling comes in as many different forms as there are children, we can see that people learn without imposed curricula. Children are naturally curious and will be driven towards learning things without being forced. Daniel Greenberg, the founder of the Sudbury Valley School, recalls stories in his *Free At Last* of 10-year olds coming to him and requesting, totally of their own volition, to be taught arithmetic. In an unschooled atmosphere, children may ask parents to teach them something or may turn to technology to find a program, app, or game that teaches the skill.

(Despite being traditionally-schooled, much of my knowledge that I use comes from playing video games growing up. My curiosity of history, writing, reading, geography, economics, politics, and basic science largely come from playing games like *Sim City 4* and *Civilization IV*.)

But unschoolers can learn about the world and the skills and knowledge necessary to operate within it in other ways — by living in it. The strongest, deepest learning comes from engaging in meaningful, voluntary behavior and actions. If a child finds fishing fascinating, they'll learn about the things related to fishing. If a child finds computers interesting, they'll naturally follow that info to what they find relevant — and this ultimately feeds other fields. Reading about history helps inform the mind about economics and philosophy. Playing *Sim City 4* can help a child learn about economics, culture, and politics. There are thousands, if not millions, playful options for education.

"Okay, fine. But what about socialization? How are children going to learn how to interact with other people if they spend their entire days at home?"

I have a friend who was homeschooled through most of his life and ran into this complaint often while a young teenager. While a parent of another child would be telling this homeschooled child who can engage in intelligent conversation with them that homeschoolers aren't socialized, they would fail to see the irony of it all.

Even taking a simplistic view of homeschooling, this is a crazy assertion for a few reasons.

1. There are plenty of homeschooling co-ops and organizations where children and adults can hang out and learn from each other.

2. Homeschool children — who aren't put in a tightly-controlled environment (a classroom from 7:30-3, shuffled off to after-school activities from 3:30-5, and then forced to do homework from 5-7) — have *more* opportunity to become socialized and interact with the world around them than their traditionally-schooled peers.

3. The alternative — traditional schooling — is intensely unlike the "real" world that comes after graduation. People are not segmented and separated by age in the workplace, sorted by last name in civil society, forced to walk with their arms at their sides in a single-file line, and expected to shut up and sit down everywhere they go.

The background assumption — that traditional schooling socializes children better than homeschooling — is absurd when you really think of it, too. The idea that people will only socialize when they **are forced to do so** is silly at best and authoritarian at worst.

"You just want kids to run around playing all the time with no structure!!"

(Well, yes, *I* do.)

The idea that every homeschooled family is just a bunch of kids running around causing chaos is a favorite strawman of some opponents of homeschooling. Unless children are poked, prodded, and cajoled into sitting down and shutting up, they'll never learn anything, so the argument goes.

There are a couple things here that are important to point out.

1. Many homeschool families, as noted above, use curricula and have schedules throughout the day. They may prefer this type of homeschooling to unschooling.

2. Children do learn from playing, and quite well. If you let them run around and play, they'll find something to focus on and learn skills with in many cases.

3. Just because structure isn't *imposed* doesn't mean it isn't there. Structure is important to an individual's life. It's *too* important to leave to schools. People need to be allowed to experiment with their lives and build structure for themselves. A one-size-fits-all approach to structure is just more likely to leave people unfulfilled and unhappy with what they've had imposed on them — and incapable of building that structure for themselves.

It's tricky to refute objections against homeschooling while also attempting to refute arguments against unschooling. Some homeschoolers like to distance themselves from unschoolers, but they shouldn't. Children are masters at learning about the world and creating structure for themselves if given the opportunity. Since it moves the locus of decision and purpose closer to the individual doing the learning, the child, traditional homeschooling is usually superior to any traditional school. When it isn't, that's usually because it's trying too hard to be like a traditional school.

AN OPEN RANT TO THOSE WHO WORRY HOMESCHOOLING DOESN'T PROPERLY SOCIALIZE CHILDREN

But aren't you worried they won't be properly socialized?

This was a question a good friend of mine posed to me during a recent conversation when I admitted that I would want my children to be homeschooled. This isn't some unreasonable person. This is somebody who recognizes that public schooling is subpar at best, recognizes that families should have the right to educate their children how they see fit, and recognizes that I am more than competent at providing an excellent educational environment.

And this is an all-too-common response to advocates of home education.

"How will they be socialized?"

"Aren't you worried they won't know how to interact with other kids?"

"Why wouldn't you want them to be around other people?"

These are usually intended as "got you!" questions and as jabs at the idea of home education. I guess in the questioners' minds, homeschoolers just sit in their house for twelve years, memorize sections of the King James Verse Bible, and learn how to weave baskets and make soap from animal fat.

I try to be charitable when usually asked this question and explain that, no, homeschooled children are usually just as, if not more, "properly socialized" (more on whatever that means below) than their peers in public schools. I try to explain that there are homeschooling groups where they can play with other children, that they interact with adults quite often, and that they can actually go do things (around other people! Scandalous!) while their peers are stuck in cinderblock cells for 8 hours of the day.

But when I lose my patience, it goes more like this...

Socialized Compared To What? Schooled Kids?

What do you mean, "are you worried they won't be properly socialized?" You mean compared to kids who go to school? Kids who go to local public schools?[3]

You're joking, right? You have to be either joking or deluding yourself.

Do you really think that sitting in a cinderblock room, being forced to learn things you don't want to learn with people you don't really know, is the best way to socialize anybody?

---

[3] I get that playing counterfactuals isn't ever really productive, but you have to be comparing realistic options, otherwise you fall into a **Nirvana Fallacy**.

Have you ever met a schoolkid? Have you ever watched how young people interact with adults outside of the school environment? They're usually awkward, kind of cold, and can't actually hold a conversation. This isn't natural.

Kids And Adults

The few you can think of actually being able to do this are extraordinary. Literally. They are extra-ordinary — beyond and above ordinary schoolkids and are only memorable because they are so rare and hard to come by. "They seem so mature!" you think when you can actually hold a conversation with them. Yes, they do, compared to their peers who are more busy picking their noses and being riddled with Ritalin to keep them from being children and actually going outside and playing.

"You can't hold the bar for socialization for children to how they interact with adults! The reason they can't interact with adults is just because they're kids."

No. It isn't.

It's because they view adults as figures not to bond with and hold conversations with like normal human beings that they view them as somebody detached and separate from themselves. They view them as authority figures, but not in the way that legitimate authority ought to be viewed (legitimate authority is earned).

At school, they come to view adults as people who read off of worksheets and State Standards for Mathematics or out of textbooks describing what John Quincy Adams did during his first term. These adults then give them work to do, none of which they have a choice in doing. Failure to do the work is met with punishment that ranges from shaming and low grades to complete removal and exiling from the only social environment (expulsion). The adults really aren't figures with whom you socialize as a child, and if you do, then you're "teacher's pet," and promptly shamed by the other schoolchildren.

At home, the family dynamic is spoiled by the school day. The few hours left for family time are devoted to eating, getting ready for bed (to get children up at the crack of dawn to do the whole miserable day all over again), and homework, leaving little time for organic family bonding. Add into this mix that children rarely are enthusiastic about homework and going to school and parents are forced to be enforcers *for the school* at home.

(This — inversion of the family dynamic so that the family is playing enforcer for the school, not the other way around — is one of the particularly nefarious effects of letting school dominate our lives. School administrators like to point out how they act *in loco parentis,* but with how much pressure is placed on parents to make sure their kids are following the schools edicts, perhaps parents are working *in loco scholis* during those few precious hours at home.)

So the children come to view their parents as an extension of the drudgery of school. Somebody has to crack the whip to do worksheets at home if the person who cracks the whip at school can't follow them home, after all. Even in the most healthy schooled families, where children don't have to be coerced by parents to do homework, the time that could be spent building a relationship between the parents and the children is eaten up by homework, after school activities, and dreading the next day of school.

It's no surprise school children are terrible at socializing with adults, then. They spent 15,000 hours of their young lives learning that adults are people who impose drudgery on them. The little time they could be spending building relationships with adults is devoted to doing this drudgery, lest they be left behind.

Homeschooled children, on the other hand, have more opportunities to interact with adults. They can build real, organic relationships with their parents, can view stranger-adults as normal people, rather than imposers-of-drudgery, and have more time in their lives to build real, organic relationships.

Kids And Kids

"That's an unfair picture to paint of schoolchildren and too positive for homeschooled kids. I mean, how are they going to socialize *with other kids*? Isn't school at least good for that?"

Again, are you kidding?

Do you remember your time in public school?

I went to a relatively good public school with few issues in way of the social scene around me, and I still view it as a pretty awful experience.

Schools are rife with bullying, drug abuse, gossip, and cliques. Schools are breeding grounds for the **very worst of socialization.**

First off, schoolchildren only primarily interact with people in their immediate age range from day one. Only in extracurricular activities and advanced classes do they have the oh-so-exotic opportunity to interact with kids who are one-to-two years older or younger than them.

Second, school is an entire world unto itself, allowing for hierarchies and social groups to develop apart from the rest of the world. There are cliques and expectations of kids imposed by other kids. There's an intense distrust of adults, so kids are left trying to navigate this social space by themselves. There is rampant drug and alcohol abuse among the older schoolchildren and this gets carried over to college, where it only gets worse.

Third, think about the kids in public schools who are the best socialized. This means that they are most ingrained in the social scene with other kids. They can navigate it well and get satisfaction out of navigating it. What happens when they graduate and are forced to interact with people older and younger than themselves? What happens when they have to move to a new area? What happens when they lose that artificial institution to navigate so keenly?

The bottom falls out.

There's a diaspora. These kids are left scrounging for connections, for meaning, and for an identity. Some can do it all over again in college and put off the diaspora for another four years, but some can't. They have to re-learn what it is like to get to know other people and form bonds and relationships. They have to do what children who aren't immersed in school for thirteen years learn to do early on.

Even for kids who are good at avoiding petty drama, bullying, and drugs, school has the negative side-effect of making them ultra-competitive to the point of myopia. You view your peers as people to constantly undercut, outdo, and are caught in a frenzy of comparing yourself to them. You view them with suspicion and distrust. High-achieving schoolchildren constantly compare GPAs, where they applied to school, and their lists of clubs in which they are officers, all while neglecting their own personal development and building meaningful friendships.

And for what? To start the process all over again.

Schooling is at best a bad way to get children to socialize properly with other children and is, at worst, cruel. Almost every case of teenage suicide is related back to problems socializing with other kids at school. Would you really want that for your children?

WTF Is Socialization, Anyway?

This all assumes that socialization is a desirable end. It assumes socialization is simply the process by which somebody can easily form organic, meaningful bonds with other people and navigate the drama and reality of the rest of their lives.

Is this the kind of socialization that schools are really designed to create, though?

The point of this open rant so far has been to ask whether or not schools are very good at socializing — and the answer is a strong no.

But what if they are really good at socializing and we've just been mis-defining socialization this whole time?

What if that processes of fearing arbitrary authority, viewing your family as agents of these authorities, and of seeing your peers as threats aren't negative side-effects of schooling, but the point of it?

The modern school system developed out of the need for a standardized work-and-war-force in 18th and 19th century Prussia (Germany) and was brought to the United States by reformers like Horace Mann, who were impressed by the German ability to apply scientific standardization to young human beings.

Thinkers like Johann Gottlieb Fichte viewed universal state-coerced (public) education as the answer to the German problem of modernity. As the church fell out under industrialization and the growth of empire, the Prussians needed something to keep their subjects working towards the goals of the state. The modern school was their answer.

Alexander James Inglis, an American education expert and contemporary of Fichte's, mirrored his concerns about creating fixed reactions to authority. In his *Principles of Secondary Education*, Inglis noted six functions of schooling, two of which, the integrating and adjustive functions, are designed to create a sense of conformity and standardization among the students and to create a fixed reaction to arbitrary authority, respectively. By placing children among their age-selected peers and by appointing teachers and administrators to look over them at all times, these ends were largely achieved in the modern school.

The socializing aspect of school, then, was designed to mimic socialization among industrial-era workers and soldiers.

Remnants of this system remain today. Think of how schoolchildren are taught to walk in single-file lines, do a military salute in the morning, and are managed by bells on strict schedules.

If this sounds conspiratorial to you, it doesn't have to. Just think of the timeline of American history, the centralization of state roles between the Civil War and World War II, and the rise of scientific management. Public schooling came to age during a time when social science was really coming into its own, too. Planners thought they could measure and standardize anything — and schoolchildren weren't exempt from that.

And the workforce wasn't, either. If the entire time you've been reading this you've thought to yourself, "tough cookies, gossip, fearing your peers, and people wielding arbitrary authority over you is just a fact of life. Look at so many workplaces!" then you'd be right. The management ideas that infected school also infected our views of work. But just because they **are** that way, doesn't mean they **have to be that way**. You can go work somewhere with a better culture or start your own company. The workforce, being less centralized and controlled than schools, has more freedom to evolve and adopt. Schools — and those stuck in them — aren't so lucky.

So maybe schools are actually very good at socializing young people. Maybe the entire process of coming to view adults as authorities to be feared and peers as problems to deal with is intentional. Or maybe not — maybe the writings of Fichte, Mann, Inglis and others are just the theorizings of madmen that coincidentally were written while the modern school was coming into its own.

Regardless, the idea that home education is bad at socializing young people when compared to its most likely alternative is laughable.

"WOULD I PUT MYSELF THROUGH THIS?"

There are plenty of different ways to organize how we think about different types of schools. We can look at whether the school is authoritarian or libertarian, to what ends the curriculum is designed, who controls the direction of learning, who makes administrative decisions, and more.

These are useful ways to think about schools in the abstract, and can be helpful for those who know what kinds of values they want the schools in which they place their children to reflect. For those who are unsure how they rank these values and what they are looking for, we may need another heuristic.

Think about the type of school you are looking to place your child or another person's child (via personal or public policy recommendation) in. Think about the structure of the school; think of the things the students would learn; think of the people who would be employed as instructors; most importantly, think of the day-to-day. Then ask yourself one question:

Would I choose to put myself through this?

If the answer is no, then you have very little grounding to place a child through it.

"Well, that's not fair. This is from the perspective of an adult, and we're talking about children. Sometimes children just have to go through certain things," may be a rebuttal.

But why is this? Do they so they can learn things? What things? Why can't they learn them in different ways? What makes childhood different from young adulthood that children suddenly have to suffer through something adults wouldn't put themselves through?

"They have to learn these things when they are young so they can pick them up and use them later. Take language, for example. How would you expect a child to learn how to read if we didn't force them to do phonics and reading exercises?"

Most children will learn the things they *need* to learn through engaging in meaningful behavior. A child may take up an interest in cars, and to be proficient at this interest will have to learn how to read, the history of the automobile (and the history of capitalism with it), modeling for cars, basic physics, mathematics, and more.

Or maybe the child will take up playing with models — model trains, airplanes, cities, etc. — and will most likely engage more deeply in this if unhampered.

Learning doesn't happen in a vacuum. Just because somebody is playing "house" doesn't mean they won't learn about math, reading, writing, home economics, building, and more. In fact, they will be *more likely* to learn from the activity, as they now have "skin in the game."

"Yeah, well, I wouldn't *want* to put myself through [type of schooling], but I went through it myself. If it was good enough for me, it can be good enough for them."

This is playing with counterfactuals. Just because you *think* it was good enough for you, doesn't mean it's the best available option among limited choices. You can't run hundreds of controlled experiments with your past self and different types of schooling to figure out if it really *was* good enough for you. If there's reasonable evidence that you can do better, and you knowingly keep your children from the system that makes them better people, that's your responsibility to bear.

Corollary: Don't Do This to Yourself

Similarly, when thinking about the future of schooling and what you would want for your children (hypothetical or not), if you find yourself saying no to a certain type of schooling experience for them, why would you subject yourself to it?

I know plenty of college-aged people who are currently enrolled in school, recognize it has huge opportunity cost and is likely a waste of money, admit they wouldn't want their own children to go, but keep trudging through it themselves.

Caring about what our future children experience is important — if not the most important thing — but respecting *ourselves* and what *we* want from life is also incredibly important. Recommendations for our children's futures can only be taken seriously by them when they are made with conviction and self-respect. Children are smart. They can recognize when an adult is really, truly lying to them and to themselves. The authority to send a child to a certain type of school is best claimed when we ourselves have taken ownership over our own educations.

Good Enough for ...

If using yourself as a foil for thinking about schooling, try to remove your position entirely from the situation. Most people think of children as some form of property or sub-person (as wrong as that it, it really is the case), so maybe saying, "would I want this for myself?" is hard to imagine. Try then, "would I put a *dog* through this?" Dogs are, after all, treated similarly to children in many families. Their routines are established by authority with little-to-no control on their ends.

Putting a dog in a cage for 8 hours every day, where it cannot engage in natural behavior, cannot even go to the bathroom without permission, will have to put up with other aggressive dogs and has no real way to deal with this, will cost the owner $10,000+, will stymy the dog's growth and could turn it into an asocial shut-in, and pretty much deprive it of the outlets it needs to flourish as a dog would be insane. Why do we do the same to children?

From a similar article written by Isaac Morehouse:

> *Just about every dog owner I've ever met would consider this an outrageously offensive rip-off that borders on animal abuse. Most of those same people beam with pride and "spirit" while putting their children through the same basic routine.* [xii]

HIGH SCHOOL IS OVER: SHOULD YOU GO TO COLLEGE?

The popular notion in the US today is that if you are a reasonably-competent, ambitious young person, you'd do yourself a disservice by not going right into college at 17 or 18.

"Going to college will increase your lifetime earnings by $1M!"

"Sure, there are people who have built successful, lucrative, happy careers without a college degree, but what're the chances that you'll be one of them?"

"You should just get your degree as quickly as possible, the rest of life can wait."

These examples of (real) advice given by peers, teachers, parents, and guidance counselors are the wrong ways to think about your education. They tend to focus on probabilities and insurances. The *probability* of making more money increases with a degree for the average person. The *probability* of needing a college degree to be successful is higher for the average person. The *probability* of being a lawyer, doctor, or accountant drastically increases with a degree.

But you aren't a lottery ticket. It doesn't make sense to think in terms of probability. Unpredictable factors can always arise that can throw off all of your best predictions, and when that day comes, you'll have to be in the driver's seat to make the decisions concerning how to proceed forward.

Forget Probability, Think About the Downside

A better way to think about education is to think in terms of payoffs and downsides.

What does this mean and why is it more useful than thinking in terms of probabilities?

Thinking in terms of payoffs and downsides means that rather than thinking first and foremost about the probabilities of some outcomes from a given decision (like going to college right out of high school), we should focus instead on making the decision that maximizes the payoff while minimizing the downside.

It's impossible to make a decision with no downside (time is scarce and every decision comes at the cost of alternative decisions), but you should focus on maximizing your upside relative to the minimized downside.

This is a better way of thinking about decisions than focusing on probabilities because it places you solely in the driver's seat of your decisions. Rather than allowing you to take a passive backseat position to probabilities (e.g., "I want to be an entrepreneur but I am more likely to make money as a doctor, oh well."), this allows you to think of your career and education as things actively in your own control. Probabilities apply to aggregates and not to individuals, anyway. In any given individual case, there are chances that some unpredictable, entirely random event ("Black Swans") could make or break you.

This isn't to say that probabilities don't matter. It simply means that they come second, not first. This allows the individual (you) to craft decisions relative to individual ability. For some people, the crutch of college is going to be needed as a period of "pre-adulthood" in order to mature into the real world after 12 years of K-12 education. For others, it will simply be a waste of time. Thinking about the probability of getting a job or an investment without considering the individual's abilities and competencies is a crude and, ultimately, misleading move and bit of career advice.

Also keep in mind that what I am saying is maximize your payoff *relative* to the minimized downside. Jumping off a cliff may provide a ton of payoff if you survive—fame, glory, exhilaration—but the downside is nearly infinite in death. In this case, the downside outweighs the payoff.

Thinking About Education in These Terms

So, what does this have to do with education? If going to college has such an upside as people claim ("$1M more in lifetime earnings!"), then isn't it the obvious choice.

No, it isn't.

Whether it's going to college or deciding to enroll in grad school or deciding to put your children in schools in lieu of home educating them, discussions on school and education overlook the downside all the time. Ignoring the fact that school makes you more risk-averse than you would otherwise be, the time alone is a huge downside.

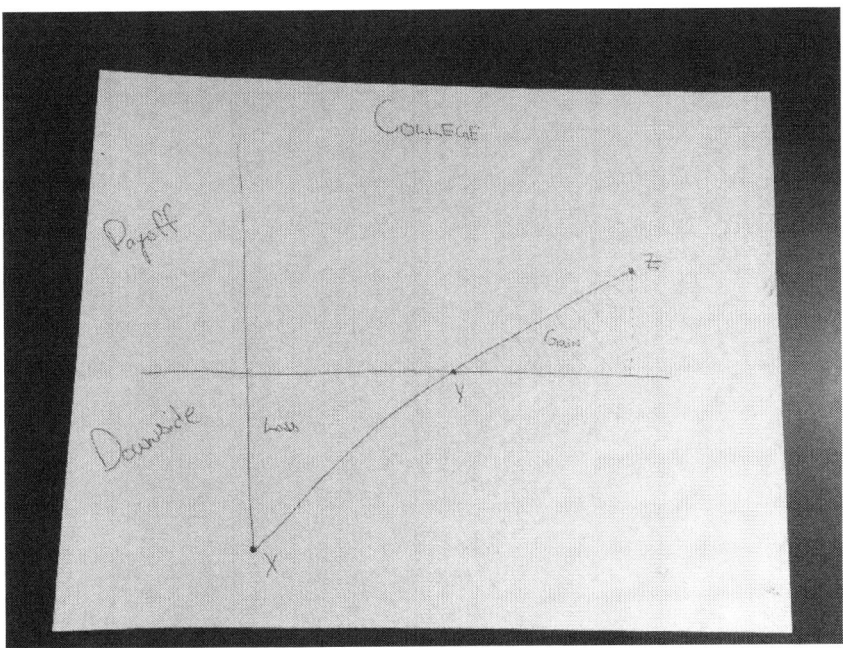

Consider this sketch:

The downside of a commitment like college is bigger than most people think.

In the case of college, your potential downsides can easily be:

- Tens (if not hundreds) of thousands of dollars wasted.

- Four years spent removed from the marketplace (you can never get that time back)

- Path-dependency and overcredentialing.
- Myriad of other issues.

At the very worst (point X on the sketch), you go and come out no better than before when it comes to prepping for a career *and* you're out of time, money, and opportunity. A good chunk of grads find themselves no better off than before when it comes for a career (point Y). The remainder land a job or career through their experiences in school (Z).

For those at Z, though, remember that this decision comes at a cost. The downside is years and tons of money spent on something that could possibly have been had without as much downside.

Consider the alternative of going into the real world and creating a learner-driven education (sketch below).

What's the worst that can happen if you spend a year in the real world first?

In this case, the downside is a small amount of time spent and potentially some money for courses, tutors, or books (you aren't locked into spending four years self-educating and it can often be done alongside other opportunities, unlike most college-based-based schooling). Should you choose to go to college or graduate school, you can (there's no law saying you have to go straight from one type of schooling to another). Worst case scenario is that you spend some time and money on classes, books, or tutors that don't get you where you want to go and you can change course (point A).

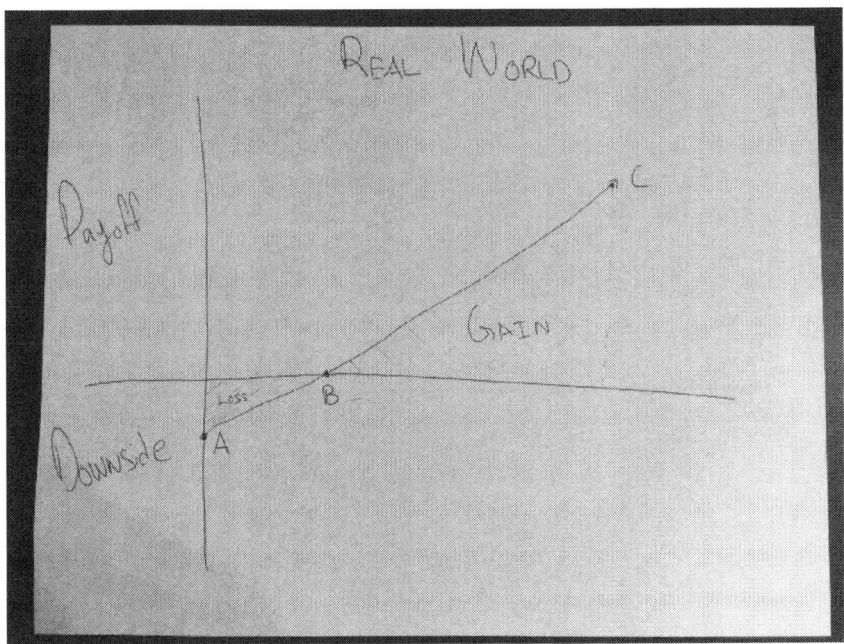

A Real Example

Rather than focusing on charts and abstract arguing about decision-making, just consider an example.

You have two young people who want to get jobs in the realm of app development.

The first goes to an accredited, four-year university and studies computer science. He spends four years and $65,000 (a modest sum compared to some colleges) getting his degree in CS and building a few projects along the way. He graduates and has to learn Objective C and Swift (neither of which are taught in college despite being the languages needed to develop iOS apps), this takes him a few months. His upside here was the credential and any brand name that can come from his university (e.g., MIT, Stanford, Carnegie Mellon are impressive brands on a resume). His downside here was the four-and-a-half years and $65,000 he spent.

The second student decides to enroll at a 10-month coding bootcamp for $12,000. He's acquainted with the basics of computer science, coding, and then is thrown right into app development. He builds a few projects along the way and is done before he turns 19. The bootcamp is taught by professional app developers and not by research professors, so the languages in the course are the marketplace-standard—he doesn't have to do any catching up when done. He's not forced to take any required Underwater Basket-Weaving classes or attend any mandatory orientations irrelevant to app development. While his competitor is busy taking these classes at 19, he's off, gainfully employed at a high-growth startup in a major city.

Who here maximized his payoff relative to the downside?

Before you get caught up in thinking about a credential he may need someday, remember that the second student could always go to college if he needs to. But given his professional goals, he doesn't need to for the time being. He's saved himself 4 years and a ton of cash while his more prestigious competitor is left out of the marketplace.

Which Will it Be?

Stop worrying about likelihoods and probabilities when it comes to your education before you consider what you're pursuing education for in the first place. Chances are, you're being pushed into decisions with huge downsides (debt, time, energy, opportunities) and mediocre payoffs. Seriously consider the fact that a $30 book may teach you more than a $7000 course, a $24 Udemy course could teach you more than two semesters, and that a $20 meal with a mentor can provide a lifetime's-worth of value.

SCHOOLING IS NOT EDUCATION; OR, A LESSON IN STATUS QUO BIAS

If you asked the average high school graduate if they feel like they learned a lot in school, they'd laugh at you. If you asked the average college grad why they went to college, they wouldn't tell you that it was to get an education, but rather to get a job. If you asked a doctor, lawyer, or academic why they went to their respective graduate programs, their answer would similarly be "so I could become a [doctor/lawyer/professor]."

Then tell somebody that you don't believe that children should be forced to sit at desks in white rooms, to walk in lines with their arms to themselves, to ask to go to the bathroom, or to learn things they find totally irrelevant to their lives. People will look at you like you've just said you want to reanimate King Tut to do a Vaudeville show for blind schoolchildren. You'll get questions like, "how do you expect them to get into college?" "How would they get to know other children and become socialized?" and "how would they *learn*?"

Despite the fact that most people are glad to admit that their own schooling adventure wasn't the primary locus of their learning, and despite the fact that they will then admit that they attended optional additional schooling not to learn, but to get past gatekeepers for other things they want to do, many find it difficult to wrap their minds around the idea that learning can happen outside of a formal classroom.

Human beings are natural learners. As higher-level beings, we are forced to learn the complex systems that govern our worlds early on, lest we be taken by the forces of nature. Language, symbols, market exchange, and the norms and mores that govern small communities like families and villages are just a few examples of things that we learn outside of the classroom (though school-creep in more and more Pre-K programs will make it that "reformers" are soon demanding we teach infants how to speak in a classroom setting), and they're incredibly complex and multifaceted things. People learn sarcasm from their friends and families — an amazingly complicated emergent quality of language. Many learn what market exchange is like by pretend-making businesses on the playground at recess, not by reading a civics textbook.

School *can* be a place of learning, but the idea that school and learning/education are synonymous and ought to be so is an outgrowth of early 20th century Progressive school reformers who were the primary advocates of crafting the language in such a way that it encapsulated everything that a common person would want out of schooling. By monopolizing school's possession on learning, anybody who existed outside of the schooling paradigm would be thought to not be learning.

The reformers established a *status quo bias* in favor of schooling. The questions that unschoolers, homeschoolers, and radical school alternative advocates (like Sudbury Schools) are asked may all be legitimate, but they are couched in the context of, "how is little Jimmy going to learn calculus[, because my status quo bias leads me to believe that he will learn it if he is in public schools]?"

Imagine if people asked the same questions of compulsory schools that they ask of homeschoolers and unschoolers.

Imagine if people gave the same scrutiny, skepticism, and questioning to public school administrators or to the teachers themselves.

The status quo bias doesn't end there. It gets worse.

Jane doesn't have a clue about what she wants to do with her life. She has gone through school for the past 12-or-so years, found herself with a high school diploma, and the question, "What now?" She decides to enroll in college, and spend the time and money figuring out what she wants to do. She flops between majors, taking classes in different areas, and eventually graduates after 5 years with a degree and tens of thousands of dollars in debt.

John knows he wants to own his own company and work for himself. He goes to college for a year, drops out, and founds a company. After struggling to build a clientele for a year, he gets some grounding, and is on the path to having a legitimate business.

Who is more likely to get the scorn of doubtful questions, Jane, or John?

"How do you expect to make a living for yourself?" "What if you can't find a job [if the business fails]?" "How are you going to learn about the world?"

It is more likely that these questions will be put towards John and not Jane. Jane will get to sail on by without much critical feedback or thought because she's doing what the status quo expects. John may very well find himself more educated than Jane at age 24. Though he may have passed up schooling at this stage of his life, he hasn't necessarily passed up education. The same questions applied to John are not applied to Jane because the status quo is to get schooled, not to get an education.

Schooling is not education. Schooling *can* be education, but even then, it is just education for a short span of somebody's life. Twelve, sixteen, or twenty years of schooling is not the end of education. Real education happens when we engross ourselves in projects that we derive meaning from and find interesting and fulfilling. If a school can do this, then it has a shot at being a place of education.

DO PEOPLE REALLY GO TO COLLEGE FOR AN EDUCATION?

Almost any discussion on the decreasing value of going to college will find an onlooker asking, "sure, but what about going to college to learn and to get an education?" The implied claim is obvious, "Even if going to college isn't worth it if you are going to get a job, lots of students actually go to get an education and to learn."

Without wandering into the weeds too far on how college is rarely the best place to get an education, the things that actually are learned at college are either outdated or not wanted in the first place, and that few college students know what they want to go learn, we can dispel the argument implied in this question pretty quickly.

Take a cross-section of your average incoming freshman for the Class of 2015 and ask them why they are going to college. A good few will tell you that they are going to learn. A larger chunk will tell you they are going so they can get a job. And another group will tell you they are going because it seems like a good experience.

There are at least three explicit reasons right here:

1. Education
2. Job/career

3. Social/consumption

We could just end this here and take students' on their word or we could delve further and see if any of these are the dominant factors for driving students to college.

Now pose this question to any of them:

"Would you go to college if it meant you would be no better off for finding a job when you graduated as you are right now?"

This would be a charitable interpretation, too, considering that college is a place where many young people spend 4 years insulated from the marketplace, learning from people who have never spent time in the marketplace, and being told what the marketplace is like. A more realistic question would be:

*"Would you go to college if it meant you would not only be no better off for finding a job when you graduated, but would actually be **worse off**, having to play catch-up for 4 years, pay off tens of thousands of dollars in student loans, an completely change your mindset from college?"*

I would wager that most of the students in your audience would say no, they would not go. Most young people are motivated primarily by the fact that they "have to" go to college in order to find a job. If college were seen as one option among many for your average- or high-achieving young person, many fewer would attend. Instead, the culture pushed on students from guidance counselors, teachers, and parents is that they *must* go in order to have any shot at being successful.

A select few students from our hypothetical cross-section would still say that they would go. Those students are probably best-off as academics.

THE FALLACY OF "AT LEAST YOU'LL HAVE IT UNDER YOUR BELT!"

Young people should just go to college now. Even if they don't know what they want to do after four years, at least they'll have a degree under their belts!

In talking with parents, young people about to go to college, and teachers, I have heard some variation on this line time and time again. The logic behind this defense essentially goes like this:

Even if a young person graduates high school and has no clue what he wants to do with his life, he should go to college. Hopefully, he'll figure out what he wants to do while he is there, but even if he doesn't, it is still better that he goes and gets a degree *in something* rather than not go at all. He can then fall back on the degree.

Something is better than *nothing*, right? The degree will at least set him apart from other people and help him get going somewhere, *right*?

It Assumes the Alternative Is Nothing

The base assumption here, "something is better than nothing," is fundamentally flawed. Behind it is this idea that if a young person doesn't go off to spend 4 years floating between classes, changing majors time and time again, occasionally drinking too much on the weekends, and then eventually being handed a degree for a major in basket weaving and an invoice for $35,000 in debt, that they will otherwise just spend their time in an empty room with saltine crackers and a glass of water for four years.

The assumption that "something is better than nothing" would be true if it weren't for the fact that four years *is a long time* and you can do a lot in that time. Even if you spend that time "flipping burgers," (which is a staple favorite reference for people trying to force college on the unsure young) at least you are getting experience of what it is like to work in a specific workplace. You could work a few different jobs, start a blog, write poetry, travel, learn a skill, go off the grid, and do so many things in four years' time.

Take a moment as the reader and think about what you knew four years ago and what you know now. Now imagine if most of this time were spent with indecision and unclear social pressures tearing you in every different direction.

The young person who is *sure* they don't want to spend some of the prime years of their life in the college setting can craft a unique plan of exploration for themselves. They can devote themselves to personal development, professional exploring, and can embrace the idea that they don't have to be lining themselves up for a 9-to-5 career immediately after high school.

The idea that the alternative is nothing is clearly flawed, but it is also deeply ignorant of the way that the world works and most people learn. Even somebody who spends these years in the most stereotypically dead-end career choice is learning more than many students drifting through generic colleges. The young person who grabs these years by the horns and bends this time to their will will leave many years ahead of their peers at 22 or 23.

It Overlooks the Cost of College

In addition to merely assuming that the alternative to college is nothing, it also either extremely downplays or completely overlooks the cost of attending college. There are two immediate costs to attending college:

- Opportunity Cost
- Price Cost

Overlooking opportunity cost is overlooking what other things could be done during four years in college. Just like imagining that the alternative to college is doing nothing, ignoring opportunity costs erases the possibility from the minds of young people that, "hey, maybe I can do something really cool when I am nineteen!"

Many opportunities — like those to fly across the country solo or to start your own business — only come along every few years and have to be embraced when they float by, lest they be lost to ever thinking, "I wonder if I had done that." For many people, the strength, will, and energy to accomplish these things is greatest between 17 and 25. After that, pressures like creating a family and getting on with professional life begin to creep in. With the additional cost of student loans, these years get even more stressful, with young people now looking to pay off loans for more than a decade or two after they graduate college.

Price cost is exactly what it sounds like. A four year school experience costs anywhere from $40,000 to $260,000+, and while not everybody pays the full price tag, this is a hefty chunk of money.

The burden of college debt pushes young people to take higher-paying but less-fulfilling jobs that they would have otherwise not taken. So, taking a few years to be a poet while working some odd-jobs is off the table. Becoming an airline pilot becomes just a dream due to low entry-level pay. And don't even think of going into commission-based fields!

But the costs of college wreak even greater havoc on the lives of individuals and families.

Middle class families pride themselves on saving up enough money for their children to attend college, even though these savings plans end up backfiring and decreasing the total financial aid given by elite universities. They beam with pride when they tell their friends, "yes, Martha and I set aside $50,000 for Johnny to attend MSU!" Johnny, meanwhile, is drifting through courses and burning tens-of-thousands of dollars per semester on "finding himself."

What if rather than wrapping up these savings funds with the promises and pretensions of college, parents just signed them over to their young-adult children at age 18 and told them they could do whatever they wanted with them?

Would some young people take it and blow it on a new car or equally-unfocused travel? Sure. Would some use it to go to college? Certainly. Some may even take it and use it as a seed-fund for a small venture or project they've been thinking of launching but lacked the resources to do so.

The important thing is that regardless of what they decided to do with the money, they would, for the first time in many of their lives, be trusted with responsibility. As with any responsibility, they may fail and suffer the consequences of their failure. They reap the benefits of their success and pay the costs of their failure. After 12 years of being pushed from classroom-to-classroom and being insulated from much of the responsibility of the real world, this would come as a trial-by-fire for many. The endpoint being that most young people would likely learn more from this experience and the responsibility entrusted with it than just being pushed through a university at their parents' behest.

Would most parents ever do such a thing? It's unlikely. They would face the ridicule of their friends and the skepticism of their family. They may have to face the humiliation of Johnny blowing $50,000 stupidly with less to physically show than an MSU degree in ancient social critical psychology.

College: Worth The Cost?

"At least you'll have a degree under your belt!" should rather be reframed as, "You'll have a degree under your belt, but will have passed up four formative years of your life to engage in some of the most interesting opportunities you'll ever have and you are now out of $50,000." When framed this way, can so many people be as comfortable in saying that college is just something you do because it is better than nothing?

THE "STEVE JOBS FALLACY" OF OPTING OUT OF COLLEGE

When a young person tells their friends and family they are thinking of dropping out of college, they may make reference to the successful college dropouts and opt-outs of our day. These men and women — the Steve Jobs, Bill Gates, Larry Ellisons, Travis Kalanicks, Richard Bransons of the world — figured they had better things to do than sit in a college classroom and little time to achieve them. They took control of their educations and their lives by making a hard decision and crafting that path for themselves.

Skeptical family shoot back, "Sure, but what are the chances that you'll be one of them? You don't want to be flipping burgers your whole life!"

And surely the prospective-dropout doesn't! They reconsider the options and make the decision based on the fear that they will be forced to scrape by from paycheck-to-paycheck if they don't have their degree.

There's an odd psychology going on here in both the minds of the skeptics and the prospects. It goes essentially like this:

If you drop out of college, you better damn well be Steve Jobs or Bill Gates. If you can't achieve that bar, then that's your own fault for walking away from a good situation.

The standard for success for somebody leaving college is raised higher than it is for the college graduate. A college grad who lands an upper-middle class job doing sales is definitely successful. A college dropout who lands a similar job is considered merely mediocre. People imagine that this person, if they had had that college degree, could have gone even further (even if they are practically at the same level as their peers with degrees).

If the college opt-out *does* reach this level of success, it is never attributed to them having left college. Even if there is good reason to think that they are successful because they had more years to deschool themselves, build a skill portfolio, and launch their own projects, the decision to leave college is only mentioned as a sidenote, "oh, and he's a college dropout!" uttered in surprise. Meanwhile, neighbors speak of the person next door who is equally successful as saying, "Oh yes, he went to Harvard, it's no surprise he's such a successful businessman." The incongruity is striking.

On the flip-side, every single failure is then attributed to not having the college degree for the college opt-out. Company goes under? *Too bad you didn't have that degree to fall back on.* Marriage falls apart? *Your wife probably thought lowly of you for not having that degree!* Got a chronic illness? *All that stress from working when you could have had your degree boost you up probably did you in!* Can't find a job at 23? *You should have finished that degree.*

If any of these things happen to the college grad, it's never because that person has the college degree. Example: Can't find a job? *Well that's just the poor economy.* Or, at best, *Well, you should have gotten a degree in Engineering instead of Business.* Though these two people — the college opt-out and

157

the college graduate — encounter the same circumstances, the college opt-out faces greater scrutiny on the point that differentiates them.

This is yet another case of status quo bias. People hold the status quo to a different standard than deviations from it and judge them by it. We view the status quo as "normal," and any deviations as inherently worthy of negative skepticism.

I call it the "Steve Jobs Fallacy." *You better be Steve Jobs if you drop out!* is a ridiculous standard to hold the college-opt out to. It'd be the same as holding the college graduate to, *You'd better be President if you go to college!* and then considering anything that comes short of that high-stature position as being failure.

Sometimes the decision to opt-out of college is the integral difference between success and failure for a given person. We can't know for certain without creating an infinite number of parallel universes in which the person does and does not go to college and makes different decisions. What we can know is that there are successful college opt-outs out there who aren't Steve Jobs, Bill Gates, or Larry Ellison. And there can be even more.

HOW COLLEGE BETRAYS OUR BEST STUDENTS

Applying to college is one of the most stressful times of life for elite students. "This is what the last 18 years have come down to," they think and are told by peers, counselors, and parents alike. Getting into a top-choice school, usually Stanford, MIT, or an Ivy League university, is the culmination of all their hard work. It's not necessarily that these schools are what's best for them, but that they, as the best students in their community, are expected to continue on to these universities.

But what if telling our best students to go to college, and especially one of *these* colleges, is one of the worst things we can do? What if we are not only making them much worse off but also society as a whole as a consequence?

This is one of the key social critiques that Peter Thiel levies against college in *Zero To One* and one that is backed-up by both anecdote and observation. William Deresiewicz's recent book *Excellent Sheep* also makes the case that top students are best off avoiding elite universities.

What has gone wrong here? What can be leading such notable figures to decry the current state of our universities? What effect is this having on our best students?

To understand this, break down the reality and the ideal of elite universities.

The Ideal

Professors and academics say college is supposed to be a place where students go off after 12 years of K-12 learning and get to engage in the materials for which they truly have a passion. Many students go into it with this academic excitement. They can finally take a class in philosophy, learn about chemical engineering, and delve into subjects they had only read books in passing on in the past.

They can participate in extracurricular activities with like-minded students, starting that club that didn't have enough interest back in high school from other students. Or they can study abroad, join a band, or really just do whatever makes them happy.

Most of all, college is seen as a place for elite students to launch themselves ahead towards their dreams. More than anything else, it's a means to an end for the elite student. Admissions officers congratulate newly admitted students every year at Ivy League institutions from Penn to Princeton about how their lives are set now that they're in the Ivy League. Students see the university as a place to gain a degree that will help them get a job in whatever industry they really see as their dream industry. For some, the skills gained in engineering, mathematics, finance, or programming are a good addition to the degree, but at the end of the day, it's that the degree is a way of getting the job that that student dreams of having.

The Reality

The reality is quite different. Students may get to take a class or two in a subject they are sincerely interested in, but once required classes are out of the way, the intense competition that many were able to avoid during high school finally kicks in. Now these students are surrounded by hundreds, if not thousands, of students exactly like them — just as driven, just as hardworking, and just as determined to win. Those who had dreams and aspirations that lie outside of the academic norm are slowly funneled into the careers the universities are best at creating.

Specifically, there are six paths that universities push students towards such fields.[xiii] These are finance, management consulting, law, medicine, Teach For America, and graduate school. When you take ultracompetitive students and place them in an environment where they *can* compete for prestigious spots in these six sectors, it's no surprise when they do. Even students who once dreamed of becoming poets or business leaders tell themselves after two years, "I'll go do consulting for a year or two, and then try something different." Many rarely do, however, try something different once they've been roped in.

It's not like these paths are anything groundbreaking, either. They are, by their mass-produced nature, less-conducive to individual action and the paths that universities are very good at pushing students towards, either because of formal On Campus Recruiting (OCR) (i.e., finance and management consulting), huge talent and recruitment pipelines (i.e., Teach For America), and undergraduate degree requirements and prestige (i.e., professional and graduate school).

So students spend four years in an institution they thought would help them reach their dreams, only to find their dreams gone by the time many graduate. No longer do they want to launch that innovative new product, pursue that crazy idea, write that book of poetry, or launch that nonprofit. Now, they tell themselves, they must be realistic and be grateful they can get a good paying job at a major firm. College has betrayed these students. These people who once had the potential to churn out world-changing products now suit-up for OCR and for their TFA interviews.

Individualists are turned into run-of-the-mill conformists. Their dreams are gone and now they just hope they get to pursue some hint of them later in life. I saw this first-hand at Penn, a school notorious for its preprofessional track. Deresiewicz saw it in his students, and Thiel in his peers. Yang sees it in his venture work. It's not an anomaly — it's part of how the system works.

Thiel, himself a Stanford graduate, puts it better than I can:

> *Elite students climb confidently until they reach a level of competition sufficiently intense to beat their dreams out of them. Higher education is the place where people who had big plans in high school get stuck in fierce rivalries with equally smart peers over conventional careers like management consulting and investment banking. For the privilege of being turned into conformists, students (or their families) pay hundreds of thousands of dollars in skyrocketing tuition that continues to outpace inflation. Why are we doing this to ourselves?*

What To Do

Fixing this process can come as at least two options. The first requires a total cultural overhaul of our higher education institutions to remove the perverse incentives and return institutions to merely being tools the students can use, not being monoliths that change the students and their desires while they are in them. This is nearly impossible. Cultural problems are multifaceted and really difficult to get a grip on.

The second option is to provide good options for elite students to follow while maintaining control over their own lives. Options like apprenticeships, fellowships, and just going and working and creating value are gaining more respect in a culture that formerly denied the honor of hard work outside of the classroom.

YOU ARE NOT YOUR MAJOR

I was recently having a conversation with a friend about what she's learned about some organizations with which she's worked. Mostly, I learned the organizations are bureaucratic, disorganized, useless-at-best, harmful-at-worst, and generally bad places for which to work. I could tell she was disheartened from just having to work with these groups.

The conversation drifted towards what she was planning on doing after she graduates. "Well," she said hesitantly, "I can either go to graduate school or I can go work for [one of these groups]."

We had just spent half an hour talking about the problems with these groups, how nobody can change them from the inside, how most of their employees are miserable, and how they are harmful towards their stated goals. I was confused as to why on earth she would want to work for one of these.

"Well, it's all you can really do with a degree in [her major]."

She's not alone. Every year, millions of graduates go into careers at companies, organizations, and agencies they don't like and don't have a passion for because they think that's all that they can do with a degree in that field. Maybe they chose the degree because they thought they could do other things "with it," or maybe because they thought that what was involved in the classes was fun and interesting. They end up trapping themselves. Thousands of dollars in debt and presented with a limited list of options by career services and websites about, "what you can do with X major," they find themselves applying to jobs they don't want.

Here's something that most people agree with on first glance: you are not your major.

Your major does not need to determine what you will do in your life. It is not your identity. Just as you are not your political beliefs, not your religion, and not your degree, you are not your major.

Most people agree with this, but most people betray it in their speech and actions. At holiday parties, on dating sites, and at family events, somebody is sure to ask a young, 18-24 year-old, "what's your major?" early in the conversation. If the answer isn't sufficiently satisfying to the questioner, it is usually followed with a "what are you going to do *with that?*"

With such pressures from friends and family, it isn't surprising that young people then start to categorize their professional options according to major.

Here's a secret: most people really don't care about your major.

On the job market, employers are more interested in your potential to create value for them. They want to know why you'll be an asset and not a liability. Once upon a time, majors were useful sorting mechanisms to help them focus in certain areas, but a candidate who can show a track-record and experience creating value

In the social world, people are less interested in what you are studying than they were in college. People are more interested in what makes you interesting. Do you play an instrument? Have you traveled anywhere exotic? Do you have passions? Hopes? Dreams? Values? "No, but I have a Communications degree," isn't a way to make friends and be interesting.

You are not your major. You don't have to limit your career choices to things that people with a degree in your field usually go into. You can use the skills, experience, and knowledge you learned elsewhere — maybe even through the acquisition of this degree — to help you land some kind of work in any number of fields. Market yourself as more than a major. Market yourself as an asset to any growing organization. Studying psychology doesn't mean you have to end up in psychology. Studying sociology doesn't mean you have to go work with an NGO or become a professor. If people are categorizing you according to your major alone, ignore them. Go create value for people so you have a track record you can fall back on.

THE COLLEGE TRAP AND THE SCHOOLED MIND

In the previous chapter, I noted how thinking in terms of your major when it comes to the job search can actually *limit* you more than it can open doors. When people start to identify as their major, they start to think that they can only do the things associated with that specific major.

This isn't just the fault of the students and the school. Relatives and friends who harangue them at dinners and nights out with, "What's your major?" and the follow-up, "What are you going to do *with that*?" as some of the first questions of interaction start to box them in.

A friend shared the post on Facebook and noted that their experience leading a student group on campus led to many more opportunities than "B.A., History" ever did. She's not alone. Many others chimed in in the comments and agreed. There's so much more to be than just your major.

There's a deeper, more-systemic issue with identifying yourself with the status of "college student," or "college graduate," or "college-bound." There's a psychological trap that people put themselves into when they think in terms of these labels and what they can do with their lives. They start to outsource their agency and identity to the schooling system.

I've written about these in more depth at the Praxis blog, and will continue to explore what it means to be schooled in the future.

American higher education is in a complete free-fall.[xiv]

Student loan debt averages out at $29,400 per student.[xv] 53.6% of all college graduates are underemployed or unemployed.[xvi] The United States has more janitors with chemistry degrees than it has chemists.[xvii] There are more than 50 universities and colleges in the United States that charge more than $60,000 per year.[xviii] And the average return on investment for degrees is in a steady decline.[xix]

And this free-fall catches very real people in its midst.

Bright-eyed and enthusiastic at 18, high school graduates are expected to enroll in the best university of their choice, lest they be forced to work hard the rest of their lives. Choosing a school that has manageable costs is important, yes, but not nearly as important as getting into a school where they can land a job making the big bucks after they get that coveted BA or BS. Students anxiously study for exams like the SAT and ACT years in advance, make sure to pad their resumes doing as many activities as possible in high school, get seen by the right members of the community, prepare those writing samples and maybe, just maybe, they'll land at that dream school.

They're told of the value of going to college, and the value of being part of an intellectual elite (while more and more students are pushed to college, thus making the elite a larger and larger class). Nobody goes for that, though. They go to land a job. Four years go by, and many leave disappointed. If they are lucky enough to land jobs, most end up working somewhere they hate, or doing something that doesn't require a degree. In short, they end up victims of the aforementioned free-fall.

If you are going to be a college student soon, you've likely heard this doomsday scenario. You've likely told yourself you won't be one of those kids who goes in with dreams and desires to change the world, only to come out a cog for a large corporate finance machine or doing something you generally hate. No! You'll go against the grain.

If you're a current college student, you probably remember being the soon-to-be college student. You probably also remember recently fretting about not landing the high-level internship all your friends yearned for, not getting that interview with Goldman, not being able to study abroad in Rome this coming year. You think the enthusiasm of the incoming freshman is cute, but in a kind of "oh, you haven't learned yet," kind of way. You probably don't remember all the things you wanted to do with your life while you were still in high school. Those things are gone. You're part of the real-world now.

If you're a recent graduate, you probably remember fretting about that study abroad, or that internship in Manhattan. You probably also wish you had gained some kind of work experience (beyond the rare work-study position), because that rejection from the job you wanted, on grounds you didn't have enough work experience, burned. You feel misled. You felt like society led you to do something you weren't entirely sure of, and now you are forced to pay the cost.

But you don't have to be the (rightfully) confused and angry recent graduate. You can regain that enthusiasm of the high school student, ready to take charge of your own life. You don't have to become part of the statistics cited above.

You get the degree to get the good job, but everybody else has the degree and the job is gone. You got it to use as a signal, but the signal is weak. You got it so you can get the job you want and have control of your own life, but without the job, you're forced to work underemployed somewhere and put your dreams on hold.

What employers need is a new signal. They need a sign that you are somebody who stands apart from the pack and is a person willing to take risks. They need somebody who *is willing to take control of their education.* I can't offer a one-size-fits-all way to seize control of your education, because that would mean you aren't seizing control of it.

Rethinking your education — and thereby rethinking the likelihood that you become one of the statistics — starts with you making the very real — and sometimes very scary — decision to seize control. For your whole life, you've waited to have permission: permission to go to this or that school; to take this or that class; to work this or that job. It is that mindset that got us to where we are today with higher education. The people who rethink higher education — whether it be their own or the system as a whole — don't wait for permission. They can have control over their own lives *without permission.*

That's what is at the core of a new paradigm of higher education — both for yourself and for society: acting without permission. Seek the job before having the degree. Take the class you always wanted to take. Build yourself up as if you were a product you're trying to sell. If you seize control now, you'll be at the helms come hell or high water.

10 BAD COMMON ARGUMENTS FOR COLLEGE

Parents, teachers, and guidance counselors happily push bright young people under them off to four years of college with the belief that it will help them grow into successful, fulfilled adults. "It's the best four years of your life!" "It's so much better than high school!" "It will help you discover yourself and set you on the path to success!" "Going to college is the best thing that will happen to my students!"

The praises flow. Parents look forward to the day that they can wear "PROUD MOM OF AN [INSERT UNIVERSITY HERE] STUDENT" t-shirt. Teachers rest on the laurels of knowing how many of their students go to college. Guidance counselors measure their school's success by the rate at which it places students at universities.

Most of the time, these young people don't question the advice and go right ahead and apply to colleges and universities without giving much second thought to it. Why should they? The people whom they have spent years either trying to formally please (i.e., teachers and administrators) or informally please (i.e., parents) have made it clear that this is the right option to please them. But sometimes one of these young people may raise their voice and question the convention. In this case, the adults in their lives are pushed to give substantive reasons for why you should go to college as a bright, high-achieving young person.

These are ten of the most common arguments I've heard adults (many of whom went to college 20-35 years ago) give young people before entering college, and why they are bad arguments.

1. College is the ideal place to learn

2. College is the best place to network

3. College is the best way to guarantee yourself some kind of job

4. College gives you confidence for the real world

5. College is fun and a great social experience!

6. College gives you access to invaluable educational resources like professors and laboratories

7. College is a prerequisite for many fields

8. College is the best environment to try different things and "find yourself"

9. College is the thing you've been working towards these past X years!

10. Going to college can only help you, not harm you.

1. College is the ideal place to learn

This argument works with a romanticized idea of the college experience.

Young people, with a hunger for truth and knowledge, will tackle the big questions of different fields with each other, sitting in socratic-style seminars and lectures hearing from luminaries in their respective fields! Professors treat their students as explorers for truth and knowledge! Students treat their professors as revered experts in highly specialized knowledge!

Except that's rarely how people treat college. Even at small liberal arts colleges, most students treat their classes as perfunctory, and many professors treat their students as obstacles, not customers (because they aren't — their parents or the federal government providing loans are, and they are several steps removed). Students who *are* looking for an ideal learning culture may find niches where they can engage in real learning. I was fortunate to land a research fellowship at Penn and work closely with a philosopher on several projects, but that kind of intimacy in learning was not the norm, especially at a large university like Penn.

How does this culture arise? If the romanticized culture is a consequence of people actually going and *wanting* to learn, engage deeply in ideas, and get a full-rounded education, then a culture that doesn't support this environment is likely the consequence of people *going to college for reasons other than learning.*

If you asked the average college-bound young person why they are going to college, the vast majority will tell you "so I can get a job." Very few will tell you it is so they can go learn in the ideal learning environment. And those who will tell you that will likely renege on that answer if you posed the following question, "Would you still go and pay the costs associated with it to learn even if you don't land a job afterwards?"

173

College doesn't meet the romanticized ideal because it is exactly that: a romanticized ideal. The reality is that it is primarily used as a mechanism for young people to go and increase their chances of landing a high-paying job at age 23 (I tackle this reason below).

Even further, more and more evidence indicates that the traditional college lecture isn't a good way of teaching people things they want to learn.[xx] While people learn in different ways, all people learn best when they are engaged in meaningful behavior that they derive value from. Just as a child is likely to ask "why?" to every assignment, college students give less attention and glean less information to and from assignments and activities that they can't engage meaningfully in. Most theory is only really engrained in people once it has been applied in practice, and only then when that practice is something they derive value from. Even if college *were* good at meeting its romanticized ideal, the romanticized ideal is only good for teaching certain things. The classroom-based model for education is itself antithetical to meaningful learning.

(Some colleges are definitely better at providing an ideal learning environment than others. Great books programs are particularly good at this and actually do stay pretty close to the romanticized ideal, but they also tend to be smaller, less-popular programs. Programs at elite research universities like Penn, Michigan, Cornell, Stanford, and others are furthest from the ideal. Professors are primarily hired to *research*, not to teach. It's no surprise then that students leave happier with their education from great books schools than schools like Penn — my own opted-out mater).

2. College is the best place to network

Even Sam Altman, one of the founders of the successful Y Combinator in Silicon Valley, says that college is probably the best place to network (though also noting that if you have the opportunity to join a startup with the potential to blow up in coming years, to take it and not go to college).[xxi] Most of the members of the PayPal Mafia went to 2 or 3 select schools. Travis Kalanick, the founder of Uber, founded his first company with classmates who dropped out of UCLA with him.

College is definitely a potential networking place for ambitious young people. Being surrounded by other people looking to achieve something in the world creates an air of importance to each friendship, and a lack of major commitments outside of school (i.e., family, job, wife, etc.) makes committing to a high-risk project easier.

But this doesn't make college the *best* place to network.

A successful network has to have several things to it. It has to be **horizontally varied** (i.e., containing people in different sectors and industries) and **vertically varied** (i.e., containing people at different stages of life and careers). This allows you to pull on people in both a large number of areas as well as a large number of stages, producing a large number of opportunities from your network.

College networks can be pretty horizontally varied, with some classmates studying philosophy, others in engineering, and yet others in economics, but they tend not to be very vertically varied. Save a handful of connections made through alumni events, most people in your college network are going to be in essentially the same stage of life as you. They are not going to be the CEOs of successful companies, or published authors with several books under their belts, or somebody even 5 or 6 years removed from you in the startup process.

If you are an entrepreneurial young person who already has an extensive network through extracurricular activities, clubs founded, or just personal connections, you can pour your resources into these to expand them even further (especially since they are likely to atrophy if you go to college). You probably already do have some vertical and horizontal variance in these networks — don't let them die out for a mediocre college network!

Even further, if you have an opportunity to do in lieu of college, like a program, fellowship, or a startup project of your own with some outside interest, you already have a framework and the infrastructure necessary to blow your network size up. Using myself as an example, my network now is infinitely more valuable than the network of some of my peers getting ready to graduate. It contains people at every stage of life in nearly every field of work, and it replenishes itself over time.

College can be a good place to network, but it definitely isn't the best.

3. College is the best way to guarantee yourself some kind of job

"Well, sure, college seems to be a huge waste of time and resources, but I need it to get *some* kind of job."

There's some logic to this, at least on the face value. Employers use college degrees as a way of weeding out certain candidates for jobs. Job candidates use it as a signaling mechanism. If only a handful of people have college degrees, and these degrees indicate that this person is more capable than somebody without it, then it makes sense for employers to look at these.

Except that's increasingly-less-so the case.

In an ideal situation, having a college degree signals to employers that you are a top-notch candidate — somebody who knows how to grind things out, do high-level research, and has a drive that cannot be challenged. In the real world, this isn't really the case. As more and more people get college degrees and more jobs require them, the strength of the signal gets weaker and weaker for students. Ideally, it signals that you are the bright, enthusiastic young person grasping a diploma after writing a complex thesis and getting 4 years of the best educational experience possible.

In reality, employers treat it as a "minimally viable candidate" signal. To them, the degree from the above-average-intelligence young person who strove to success through four years of college means just as much (or as little) as the degree from the guy who showed up hungover to class (when he showed up) and partied 4 nights a week.

The people who have the most to *lose* by going to college are the people of above-average intelligence/work ethic. Their degree signals the same thing as the person of below-average intelligence/work ethic who goes.

Even if you don't buy all this about the decreasing strength of the signaling power of the degree, just look around at the number of people with college degrees working jobs that don't require degrees for your evidence. There are more janitors with chemistry degrees in the US today than there are chemists.[xxii]

Meanwhile, jobs that *don't* require college degrees see gains in demand and (therefore) salary. Crane operators can make upwards of $50,000 a year for small operations, and operators in major cities have been reported to make up to $500,000 a year.[xxiii] Marketing agencies are happy to hire candidates without college degrees if they have experience and know how to write good copy. Even major airlines, pushed to ameliorate a coming pilot shortage, are happy to hire candidates without college degrees.[xxiv]

The entrepreneurial young person shouldn't even have to worry about this argument for college, though. They know that whatever comes their way, they'll find a way to pay the bills. Who cares about landing a corporate job that requires a BA to apply when you have 15 ideas for companies you want to launch?

If you do want to pursue this entrepreneurial path, sometimes dropping out or foregoing college altogether can be a more powerful signal than sticking it out.

(And honestly, who would want to work for a company that's so stodgy that it wouldn't budge on the BA requirement for an otherwise-well-qualified candidate?)

4. College gives you confidence for the real world

Some people — especially Baby Boomer parents — will attribute their success (and oddly enough, rarely their failure) to the fact that they got a degree from an elite university.

"I wouldn't be where I am today if it weren't for my time at college!" they may proclaim. Or they say that the challenges and opportunities they had to cope with through college prepared them to go confidently into the real world.

It's entirely possible that working through 8 semesters of grueling classes, building camaraderie through greek life, and just generally putting up with the strife of college may prepare you for the real world and to approach it confidently.

But *actually dealing with the real world* is even more likely to give you the confidence to tackle it. The great thing about being young is that people expect you to screw up, regardless of student status. If you do screw up, no big deal, but you will feel more incentive to do better than if you were isolated in the college campus.

Some of the video games I played growing up had "practice" or "arena" levels or features where you could go around with infinite lives and try different things. Sometimes you would screw up and face a minimal penalty for it. The point was so you could try things out here, get a feel for them, and then go play the game having gotten that feel. This sometimes worked when I was stuck in the Story Mode. What was much more likely to help me get my shit together and get through a rough patch of the Story Mode was *actually failing at the Story Mode*.

You spend the first 12 years of your schooling career on practice mode. The sooner you can get into Story Mode and try, try, try again, the better. It's going to be hard regardless, so why put it off?

5. College is fun and a great social experience!

You can hear it now: some dad, beer or cocktail in hand, chortling and saying, "College was the best four years of my life!"

Imagine the crowds of students at a college football game, playing in the marching band, partying it up at a frat house or with a few friends in the dorm. The sexiness of the college social scene is the subject of hundreds of American comedies. It's got an aura around it.

Here's the thing though: this isn't an argument for college at all. It's an argument for the social scene around it. Most of this can be had without paying 4 years of your life and tens of thousands of dollars to universities and colleges. You can go to college football games. You can attend college parties. Make friends with a few college students and save yourself $25k that they aren't if you are really looking for the college experience.

If you are looking for team spirit and the joys that come with that, just look around yourself at March Madness. The teams people cheer for are rarely their alma maters, but rather teams *they choose* to like.

If it is just a sense of closeness with other people while working towards a common goal that you are looking for, join a program or fellowship for college opt-outs, start your own startup, or go join a growing one.

What is also oftentimes left unsaid when somebody says, "College was the best four years of my life!" is that that's because the subsequent years haven't been in their control. College-age is the first time many young people have the freedom to build their own lives. Sometimes they choose to go to college and exert that freedom (and much of the time older people push them towards it). They play with this freedom for 3, 4, maybe 5 years, and then set themselves back on a path where they put that freedom on autopilot. They fall into a job that they don't hate, but that they also don't exert their primary control over. They can't feel camaraderie with their coworkers because they don't really choose their coworkers. The people they hang out with and work around just happen to be people who are physically close to them.

By choosing to take control of your education and your life, and maintaining that control, you can also control who you socialize with much more easily. You don't have to worry about 18-22 being the best social years of your life, because if a year isn't your best, it's considerably easier for you make it so.

6. College gives you access to invaluable educational resources like professors and laboratories

Colleges like to show off the shiny new laboratory they built last year and named after some trustee, or the new floor of the renovated library, or how many professors they have listed with fancy endowed chairs. They like to list these things in their marketing materials because it works on prospects.

Thankfully, many of the resources that were once concentrated in places like universities are now dispersed across the globe thanks to the Internet. Entire libraries are now available online. Lecture slides from Ivy League universities can be found with a simple search of Google. Yale Open Courses, Coursera, and Khan Academy all bring lectures and resources to anybody who has a modem. Much of the *knowledge* concentrated in universities has been dispersed.

Even still, the idea that college is the only place to access human resources like professors and their colleagues is one that may be true if professors just hid in caves all day, came out to teach, write a little, and went back to their university-owned caves. The reality is that they actually interact with people in the real world like others do. They attend summer and weekend seminars, write books, have email addresses (and sometimes respond to emails sent to that address!), and can be contacted. Sometimes they contract with independent programs to do guest lectures or exams. They may even appear on the radio or on television to talk about a topic and then give out contact info.

The point is that college isn't the only place to access the human knowledge in professors. Many professors are flattered to receive emails from enthusiastic young people inquiring about work they are doing. There are ways to gain access to them if somebody really wanted to build this close partnership with a professor.

Capital resources provide another kind of challenge. While knowledge can go anywhere that somebody has a browser on a smartphone or laptop, laboratories are much harder to turn into bits and bytes.

Thankfully, university-level laboratories are mostly only useful to those with niche interests in high-level research. As globalization drives the cost of equipment production down, and as more and more universities look to update their equipment, smaller companies find themselves coming into laboratory equipment once thought unimaginable for a company. Even further, with the growth of biotech, startups build partnerships with these capital-laden universities to gain access to their resources. So it isn't entirely off-limits to those outside universities.

This capital restriction raises a good point about the ease of innovation for somebody lacking heavy resources (like money or political power), though. While anybody with a keyboard an API can design the next million-or-billion dollar app and launch it on to the Internet, it is much harder to invent a new form of steel, or a line of nanobots, or a new drug. The barriers to entry are kept within select institutions like venture-backed startups, universities, and government agencies. If you are looking to innovate in a hard-science field or like an Ayn Rand character out of *Atlas Shrugged*, you may be best served looking at ways into some of these institutions.

7. College is a prerequisite for many fields

It's no secret that it is impossible (or very, very, very hard) to practice medicine, law, or accounting without an MD, JD, or CPA, respectively. It's hard to tell somebody to completely forego higher schooling if they have a dream of being one of these things.

Similarly, while being an intellectual doesn't require any degree at all, being an academic professor is best served with a PhD (though, increasingly, as is being a Starbucks barista).

The thing is, though, this is a very short list of very specific careers.

If you are *very* sure that your life-plan for success must include being in one of these fields, then you will likely have to pursue college first (my advice then is to do it as cheaply and quickly as possible with AP credits, dual-enrollments, and merit scholarships).

But if your life-plan doesn't include one of these things or working for a massive corporation like Morgan Stanley, then you may be better served by going and getting experience doing something first. Marketing agencies would happily hire somebody who dropped out of college and spent two years learning marketing copy and digital marketing strategy before they would hire somebody with a marketing degree. Sales can only be learned by joining a sales team, putting together a deck, and building a Rolodex. The startup process that every founder has to go through can be written about and have classes taught on it, but it is different for each person.

If you want to do any of those things or the myriad other options that don't require a degree, taking the time, money, and resources to pursue the degree when you *could* be doing something else will actually harm you in the long run. The degree requirement is a barrier-to-entry for some fields, but *getting* one can also be a barrier-to-entry in others.

8. College is the best environment to try different things and "find yourself"

If you ask most young people why they are going to college, they will tell you so they can land a job. If you then push them on what job they are looking to land after college, many — even college seniors — won't be able to give you a straight answer. They went to school because 1) they "had to" to get a job (because this is what they'd been told growing up), and 2) to figure out what kind of job they wanted to do.

Turns out that the best way to "find yourself," just like the best way to get confidence in #4 above, is to actually go out into the world and try different things. Even the colleges that offer study abroad programs, consortiums with other universities, and 657 majors and concentrations form 19th Century Analytic Philosophy to Micro-bio-engineering to Underwater Basketweaving can only offer you so much. A college admissions packet may make it seem like the university offers a varied and interesting experience, but those experiences are still just a very small selection of the experiences available to an 18 year old American today.

I used to laugh at people who would tell me that they wanted to backpack through Europe or Asia. I still don't think it's necessarily something I would do for myself, but if it is taken correctly as an opportunity to engage meaningfully with the world around you, it can be an infinitely more interesting and enlightening experience than the average 4 year college trip.

Here are 10 things you can do in 4 years that are more likely to help you find yourself than dabbling through courses at college and are probably all cumulatively cheaper than college:

1. Start a blog and commit to contributing to it on a regular basis that you set for yourself.
2. Commit to reading a certain number of books every month
3. Learn a new language
4. Travel abroad by yourself for an extended period of time
5. Learn boating/flying/motorcycle riding and the basic maintenance required for each of these.
6. Learn three new digital skills through local courses, MOOCs, or programs like Codecademy.

7. Learn three new soft skills like public speaking through local groups like Toastmasters.
8. Become certified in a profession, like real estate
9. Move to a new city
10. Join a startup team

All of these things are considerably more likely to lead you do "find yourself," figure out what you like, what you don't like, and how you can achieve a balance in life doing mostly the things you like than drifting through college for 4 years like many students do ever would.

9. College is the thing you've been working towards these past years!

If you've been brought up knowing that others think you are smart, you probably have either crafted much of your schooled life towards building that ideal college application, or have had others structure it in this way for you.

For me, all of high school was a testing ground to see whether or not I could get into an elite university. I even told my parents, after being admitted to one of my first-choice schools, "this is what I have been working for all these years!" And I hear teachers and parents say the same line to young adults considering foregoing college.

The problem is that this is fallacious thinking.

The idea that you should do something because you have already devoted so many resources to doing so is called the sunk cost fallacy, and it permeates our thinking about college.

Maybe you did devote 4 or more years of your adolescence to the pursuit of an elite college admission letter. Maybe you gave up nights to study for the ACTs and the SATs. You threw money at extracurricular activities, classes, and programs that you knew would give you *that* edge you needed to get in. And what? You're going to walk way from all of those resources being used?

Those resources are gone. They aren't coming back. Those nights you spent, those weeks at camp, those dollars on exam prep won't come back if you go to college or if you don't. Don't let yourself fall victim to the sunk cost fallacy.

Just like a person who is in a relationship that is going downhill thinks to themselves, "Well, I spent all that time building this relationship, and all that money on dates, and flowers, and gifts...maybe I should stick with it," it is just as bad an idea to apply the same logic to your career and life-path over the next 4 years.

Get out now, lest you fall into an abusive relationship with college.

10. Going to college can only help you, not harm you.

Admission day comes and you find out that you have been admitted to the elite university that your parents and you(?) have been striving towards. "The world is your oyster! It is my pleasure to have reviewed your application and to admit you to our class!" reads the standard admission letter.

In addition to that, you get a hefty financial aid package that makes it that you won't have to go into debt to complete a degree from this school. You've done it!

But you decide you'd rather not go. You feel that you could rather spend your time learning the things you want to learn with the resources available, launching a few projects, and taking control of your education and your life in a way that you have never been able to before now.

You explain every reason why you don't want to go and your parents and teachers and counselors shoot back, "Why not? It can only help you at this point! It won't even cost you a dime!"

This is the key point here. While you are explaining to them all the opportunities you would have if you don't go to school, they forget that included in the cost of attendance isn't just the monetary cost, but also the opportunity cost (the value of the next-best options). Not only could you earn money over these four years, but you could also set yourself on the path to experience, skills, and launching your own venture while your peers are scurrying to finish midterms.

A second danger in the schooled mind...

There is also a very real sense in which continuing schooling immediately after 12 years of schooling *can* harm somebody. People who spend many years and hours being trained to succeed in a very specific system that rewards very specific actions like schools do find themselves having a hard time adapting to the world outside of school. They've come, largely through no fault of their own, to view the world as a series of assignments, tests, due dates, and clear expectations outlined in the student handbook.

This way of viewing the world — what I call "the schooled mind" — only gets worse in college. There is some liberty allowed in choosing classes and in attendance of these classes, but generally speaking, students are still held to assignments, due dates, and clear expectations. They fall into at trap of expecting the world to be like this.

Succeeding in an ever-changing world that demands that more people view themselves as entrepreneurs than ever before requires a thorough period of deschooling. Some of the best students at universities can be the worst employees for small organizations. They are too schooled. The person who can deschool themselves early, develop an organic view of the world as a place where value-adds have to be identified and created by the individual, not assigned by a manager, will be leaps and bounds ahead of the well-schooled student with a degree from an elite university.

These are just a handful of the bad arguments for going to school, and just a small sample of potential rebuttals to them, that I've encountered in my time of talking to high school students, college students, teachers, counselors, parents, and mentors. At the end of the day, the important thing is for the young person to be able to take control of their life as their own and to be in the driver's seat of their education. Parents can be useful inputs, and may have serious say if they are financing the experience — but young people need to embrace the radical freedom they can seize for themselves at age 18 or 19 and make the most out of it. Turn off the autopilot, take control, and go build something great.

Section 3: Schooling And The Real World

The illiterate of the 21st century will not be those who cannot read and write, but those who cannot learn, unlearn, and relearn.

Alvin Toffler

DESCHOOLING MYSELF

I was by all means an excellent student. I excelled at elementary school, middle school, and high school assignments. I always had an excellent report card, participated in several major extracurricular activities, and held down some kind of job when legally allowed to do so. But I also hated school.

I didn't hate *learning*, but I hated the idea that I had to fill out arbitrary test preparation forms through 11th grade and spend my time on assignments dedicated to preparing me for an exam I knew I'd do fine on anyway. Most of my teachers hated it too, but, like me, relented themselves to the fact that this is just the hand we had been dealt.

For the most part, I was an excellent student not because I simply loved the idea of being an excellent student qua student, but that being a good student meant *freedom*. If you got good grades and did well on the exams, you could afford to leave class a few days a month to go work on a project you got more personal satisfaction out of (for me, this included musical projects, newspaper, pet projects, and some of the clubs I was involved in). Nobody would have an incentive to hold you back. If you caused some worry for the school, they'd be more skeptical.

I found I learned best and most when giving myself over to those projects. Editing from newspaper, leadership and mathematics and history from music, history and public speaking and rhetoric from student congress, and philosophy and rhetoric from forensics are just a few of the areas I learned more from being engaged in a project tangentially related to them.

I was also a good student by college admissions standards, too, and consciously so. "College is better than high school. You get to choose your own classes and get ownership over what you do," was the general theme I had internalized. "Better than high school," was the thought, and that meant, for me, "freedom."

I found that this was largely not the case, and was just high school with more opportunities to engage in licentious behavior and pay your life savings for it. But I had been schooled, so I figured I'd deal with the system from the inside and get the most out of it. Until I couldn't anymore. My tunnel-vision from trying to escape the standardized-testing world of high school had schooled me itself. Everything must be done to an end. I saw it in my classmates, too. "Oh, you're doing X club? Yeah, that looks great for OCR (on campus recruiting)!" "I don't particularly like Y activity, but I know it will help ingratiate me with the recruiters from Z firm." And on and on, *ad nauseum*. The lack of freedom associated with public, standardized schooling had been replaced with a lack of freedom in the culture of what people pursue and why.

I had forgotten the joy and flow experienced when engaged in an activity for itself, as I had in middle school (and, unfortunately, many of these merely came to be seen as resume-builders for college as I got into high school, even if my original engagement was one of fulfilled exploration). I had started to become schooled, and the prospect of going down that path was not something I wanted.

Being schooled isn't just being somebody who has spent 15 years in schools, working on exams (whether they be standardized exams given by the school or by the College Board). Being schooled is being in an anxious mindset, viewing each part of life as just one level before achieving objectives to level-up to the next stage (e.g., 9th into 10th grade, high school into college, college into graduate school). Being schooled is a mindset of "what assignment is next?"

Juxtapose this against a deschooled mindset, where there is no "next assignment" because life brings itself meaning out of the activities you do. You may be working towards projects, but you don't artificially divide your life into due dates, graduation dates, certificates and awards. You can rest on the laurels of your achievement when it has a track-record of actually having created value somewhere, not merely because you checked off the requirements on a list.

Being deschooled may be a step to existential fulfillment — making it easier and less-anxious once again to engage with math, writing, and other subjects that were once spoiled for somebody by relentless schooling.

For me, deschooling myself is a constant process. Removing the imposed structure of schools from one's mind, and questioning those where they are clear and obvious in the physical world, are key steps to this. More than anything else, it has been integral to reclaiming the flow and fulfillment I've felt doing those things I love.

THE SCHOOLED MIND

The schooled mind is a consequence of imposed visions and definitions for the future. It crowds out the vision of the deschooled mind — the vision of the student left alone from imposed systems.

The schooled mind is simultaneously indefinite, while being the consequence of limitedly definite systems.

The schooled mind is constricted in the options with which it operates. If options A, B, C, and D are all the ones on the test, then option E isn't on the table.

The schooled mind is systematized and managed. English is a subject separate from Government, which is separate from Algebra, separate from Statistics, from Chemistry, History, Economics, Music, and from "the real world."

The schooled mind is obsequious. It defers to power and to authority. It isn't the role of the schooled student to speak up and speak out. It is the role of experts to imbue knowledge upon the not-yet-schooled.

The schooled mind is fragile. Even in classes designed to benefit from disorder and chaos, these are separate experiences from the schooled process. It is damaged by disorder.

The schooled mind is exogenously motivated. Grades, study halls, recess, gold stars are all incentives to do better on things from which the schooled student doesn't inherently find meaning.

The schooled mind is indefinite. "Let's get to the next level," "let's get an A on this next exam," "if I just get into my top school, that's what will be the goal here." Any individual values it is motivated by are those values considered possible options within the schooled system. The ability to build a definite vision for the future is off the table unless the schooled student has an option to embrace the deschooled alternative for their own future and then choose schooling if that is necessary to reach their individual vision.

THE DESCHOOLED MIND

The deschooled mind is definite in its focus and purpose. When something that is worth pursuing is found, the deschooled mind can focus on it with relentless effort and focus. It isn't pushed in a million different directions by the institutions around it.

The deschooled mind is creative. It can approach the same problem from multiple perspectives. It doesn't view problems as necessarily constructed with a given purpose in their solution. The deschooled mind is not constructivist.

The deschooled mind is antifragile. It benefits from the disorder of the world. While the schooled mind is naturally resilient-at-best and fragile-at-worst, the deschooled mind is antifragile-at-best and resilient-at-worst.

The deschooled mind is playful. It is capable of taking multiple situations and working with them at the same time, without viewing one as being an all-or-nothing game when it really isn't.

The deschooled mind is confident. It isn't built on the affirmation and accolades of other minds as its foundation. It doesn't need to wait for somebody to say "go" to go and succeed on a task or project.

The deschooled mind is innovative. By being given to viewing problems from multiple perspectives, the deschooled mind can see secrets more easily than its schooled counterparts.

The deschooled mind is self-willed. By finding its primary drive for purpose and meaning in activities from itself, the deschooled mind is more easily given to finding existential fulfillment than the schooled mind — a mind that operates largely within the context of moving to the next pre-defined level.

The deschooled mind is essentialist. Since its activities are chosen for its own sake and reasons, it must filter through the noise of what is pushed on it. Where the schooled mind is given to doing things because they are assigned or expected, the deschooled mind operates freely outside this paradigm.

YOU GRADUATED! NOW DESCHOOL YOURSELF

Congratulations, Class of 2015! You've completed your higher education journey and graduated from college! Sure, you may be the most indebted in history (until 2016, that is),[xxv] and there's a good chance you'll be employed in a position that doesn't actually require a degree,[xxvi] but you went for the gold that was expected of you for success and are now ready to take on the world! If you haven't applied yet, you are probably thinking over what kind of position you want as your first job. You may anxiously peruse "Required Skills" lists and think of ways you can twist those all-nighters popping between Facebook and your required Intro to 15th Century Basket Weaving of the African Diaspora textbook into "SMB Prospecting" and "Strong Verbal and Written Communication."

Regardless of the job you apply for and its required skill set, you will need to do one very important thing if you want to succeed as a young professional in the 21st century: deschool yourself.

Unless you want a job that discourages innovation, entrepreneurial thinking, an efficient mindset, and the ability to strive towards goals without getting distracted on resume-building credentialing and fluff, deschooling yourself is the best single thing you could do in the professional development arena to set yourself apart from your peers.

To understand what deschooling yourself entails and why it is so important for success as a young professional, first look at what being schooled means.

After 16 years of sitting in classrooms, turning in assignments, working to deadlines established weeks in advance, planning out your path semesters-early, and jumping through hoops to move to the next level in the game (i.e., jump through the hoops to get from middle school to high school, high school to college, college to your graduation), the idea that what matters in the world is the value you produce for other people comes as a shocker to many.

It doesn't matter how much time you spent sitting in meetings, on conference calls, working on that quarterly report late at night, if you don't actually create more value for your employer or for your customers than they are willing to pay you, you won't be successful with them (let alone rise through the ranks to the next level in the game like before).

Even worse, you won't have a rubric or a syllabus set out in front of you to explain how you can create this value. You won't have office hours. You won't have a tutor you can pull aside and ask for advice. You will have to figure out through a process of complex and oftentimes conflicting signals what your supervisors, friends, colleagues, and customers want.

You may get passed-over for a promotion for the guy who comes from a considerably worse school or hasn't been at the same company as long. You may find that even though you followed your B-school textbook down to the tee, your business is floundering.

You may find yourself killing the assignments you get for work but not being able to find value to create in between, sitting around waiting for the next assignment to come your way (think back to high school when if you finished your in-class work early you could read your book or daydream until the end of the period).

And employers notice. One of the biggest hurdles of training a new employee is getting them out of the schooled mindset. Getting them to realize that there is no assigned reading, there are only occasional assignments, and it is up to them to figure out how to get to the next step in their career is burdensome for employers. An employee who just sits around waiting for the next thing to do is an employee whose habits are hurting the team.

The fact that you have these little habits — waiting for assignments, looking for obvious rubrics and the way to the next level, feeling a tinge of resentment to those who get ahead when you are the one who has put in more time/work/has more credentials — doesn't make you a bad person. It's to be expected after spending the entirety of your memorable-life thus far in a set of institutions that reward this kind of behavior. What you have to figure out now is how to do away with them and cultivate habits to succeed at navigating the open systems of profit and loss and value creation in the marketplace[4].

Deschooling yourself is cultivating these habits. It's moving from a mindset of "when's the due date?" and "what's on the

---

[4] "The marketplace" isn't something just for entrepreneurs and businesspeople. It's something for all of us. Given that people exchange not only money but also time, favors, and energy when they see themselves as being able to get something of equal-or-greater value out of the exchange, "the marketplace" can refer to navigating relationships with investors, entrepreneurs, and business people, but it can also refer to landing your poetry to be featured in a magazine, or how to barter with a local during your next big bike trip, or any number of things that involve interacting with people outside of a schooled setting.

test?" to "what other projects can I undertake and complete with the time I have?" and "where can I add value?"

This process can differ between individuals, but it starts with one simple truth:

The world owes you nothing except for the value you create within it.

You are not owed a promotion because you have been at the company longer than your colleagues. You are not owed profit because you opened a business. You are not owed page views because you put a lot of effort into your tumblr.

Start with this truth and work from there. When you find yourself lagging behind your goals and expectations, look to where you can create more value. Look to where you can hack the systems set up in a thoroughly-schooled world.

Learn a skill set you didn't study in school. Just because you didn't study coding doesn't mean you can't learn it. You don't need an English degree to learn how to write better.

Read books you didn't have time to read. You don't have to wait until summer to read about what interests you. Pick up a novel and enjoy it alongside a book that helps you at what you do.

Do things that aren't assigned to you. The biggest secrets are those that nobody knows how to design assignments to find. Go find them.

Don't expect syllabi and finals. Every day is a final.

Know that the hoop-jumping of your student years only goes so far. If you want to really get ahead, you have to tear down the hoops entirely.

DESCHOOLING ISN'T THE OPPOSITE OF STRUCTURE — IT'S THE HEIGHT OF IT

I've never let my schooling interfere with my education.
— Mark Twain

I was fortunate enough to speak at an event in San Francisco this summer about the necessity of deschooling yourself for leading a successful life. The audience consisted of young intellectuals and entrepreneurs who might want to step off the traditional school-to-cubicle conveyor belt and try different approaches to education. They were generally open and amenable to what I talked about. I discussed my own experience leaving school after being a top student, trying to develop a work habit that allowed me to be continually productive, and what struggles I and others had had with deschooling ourselves.

Almost every question came back to the same issue: structure.

"Don't you think most young people need structure in their education?"

"Isn't structure a good thing for people?"

"What kind of life can you lead outside of a structured environment?"

The thing is, I don't disagree with the premise behind these questions. Structure is incredibly important for individuals to lead free and fulfilling lives. In fact, structure is so important that it can't be left to one-size-fits-all models in schools.

These questions assume that without an **imposed structure** on your life, you can't have structure. You have to have somebody telling you when you have to study X, what you have to do to do Y, and a certain path that must be imposed on you to get you from a kid to a productive member of society. Though the questioners didn't mean it this way, this assumption takes an inherently pessimistic view of people. It views them as being so listless, so self-absorbed, and so short-sighted that they couldn't possibly lead productive lives without imposed structure. Defenders of schooling like to mock dissenters for wanting kids to just play all day instead of learning (despite strong evidence that play is a better use of time).

This is hardly the case and the confusion with deschooling with the complete removal of structure stems from this misunderstanding.

Deschooling isn't the complete removal of structure in our lives. People need structure. Without some kind of narrative to build his life around, man has a difficult time moving forward, being happy, and being able to set ends and develop paths to develop them. Schooling creates the facade of **created structure** through a system of imposed structure. It takes many people and puts them down a limited number of paths. This makes people believe that they have structure in their lives and are forming narratives. It isn't until a particularly bumpy part of life — a corporate downsizing, a close death in the family, or some other large event that shakes their identity — that they realize that he hadn't yet built the structure he needed for his life. He's come to equate process with substance; degrees with knowledge; and graduations with experience.

Deschooling is stepping outside of this system of imposed structure and engaging in the individual process of creating your own structure for yourself. This isn't easy, especially in a thoroughly schooled society. The individual, used to getting up and going on a clearly defined schedule from hour-to-hour and day-to-day and semester-to-semester, is now forced to create a schedule for himself. He's forced to do this while simultaneously watching his friends and family go through the same system of imposed structure.

There are at least three areas that we must focus on if we want to allow the process of finding **created structure**. The first is to have **focus**. Find what you are good at and focus on it relentlessly. If you can't do that, remove what you are bad at and focus on what is left over. Do not waste time on the unnecessaries. This allows us to figure out where we want to be in a few years and develop a path to get to it. Too often school leaves us with the mindset of, "well, I want to get into Penn. Then I'll go to a top program from there. Then from the top program I'll get a good job," but never forces us to ask why we are going for that job in the first place. We focus on the process more than we focus on the substance and where the process takes us.

The second area to cultivate is **creativity**. Creativity isn't simply being able to make a nice painting or write a pleasant creative story. Creativity in our own lives means so much more than this. It means being able to see ourselves as being multifaceted. You aren't *just* a law student. You aren't *just* a doctor. You aren't *just* an entrepreneur. This is important for the individual's ability to craft identity over a lifetime. If a given project or path fails, she can pivot to another path, creatively taking her talents and passions elsewhere and not getting stuck in the rut of viewing herself as a failure. It's no secret that schools have a propensity for crushing creativity — read any number of studies about the importance of the arts, music, or creative work outside of assignments and tests — but it also has a much more sinister effect on creativity in the grander scheme of human knowledge. By teaching to tests and mandates, school removes the importance of creative knowledge seeking from the human experience. We aren't pushed to ask the big questions as often and must turn our attention to what we currently know. Without this mindset, humans are free to ask "why not?" more often. When they ask it in school now, the answer comes down to little more than, "because it isn't on the test."

The third area is to develop an attitude of **play**. One of the most important things I've internalized over the past 2-3 years is that life is ultimately a series of games and should be seen as such. These games can be played many times over. If you worry about a given path too seriously, you focus more on the process of going about that path than about developing the right mindset to enjoy it and to find it meaningful. This isn't just a self-help platitude, either. Having an attitude of play helps us learn more easily. When we view our work as not drudgery but as something enjoyable and meaningful, we find new ways of accomplishing tasks. Play is a central tool in the human being's cognitive toolkit for learning new processes. Without it, we're not much smarter than machine learning AI.

Focus, creativity, and play give us the tools and mindset necessary to create structure for ourselves outside of school. By removing the barriers of imposed structure and by engaging more deeply in our human potential as creative problem solvers, we can not only create meaning and structure for ourselves outside of a system of grades, tests, assignments, and bureaucratic career paths, we can also unleash a new attitude of pushing the boundaries of human knowledge.

Deschooling isn't the removal of structure from our lives. It is the process of reclaiming our rights as individuals to determine what that structure ought to be for ourselves. We don't need a school board or a Secretary of Education or a Vice Provost to tell us.

YOU ARE NOT A PRODUCT OF YOUR COLLEGE

There's almost always some article going around on Facebook about the "best colleges for ROI" or "the best majors for ROI." These usually don't get to me too much despite being entirely grounded in the wrong logic of "investing" in something that is almost entirely signaling and can't really be compared to investing in stocks or a house or some tangible good. A recent one from Forbes called "The Grateful Grads Index," featuring the top 50 colleges for "Return On Investment" keeps popping up, though.

This one kind of got to me.

Why? Because it implies that these graduates had better be grateful to the institution they attended for their success (assuming ROI on college is a good measure of success). It robs them of much of their own agency in becoming the successes they are and attributes it to the institution. It says, "You are successful because you went to [Stanford/Yale/Penn/Michigan/Harvard/ MIT]. You should express gratitude." It implies that they were nothings, nobodies, no chance at success until their institutions came along and made them into the Sergey Brins and Elon Musks that they now are.

That's all ridiculous.

College Is Primarily Signaling, Not Human Capital

For what are the graduates supposed to be grateful? If it is some kind of knowledge or skills the universities endowed upon them, then this is a fundamentally flawed assumption. The assumption isn't rare, either. Grads enter as a ragtag group of college freshmen and come out an early version of their later-successful selves. It's no surprise that this is an assumption, either. Colleges repeat this in all of their recruitment and marketing material. "This is where you'll learn the skills to equip you for a successful life," some quote from some alumnus says on the brochure. Commencement speakers proclaim that it was only by attending their institution that they got to where they are today. Politicians and their followers announce loudly that "more education" is what is needed to improve the economy, despite most young people admitting that what they learned in college is not useful in their jobs.

This is because college is not about learning knowledge, gaining skills, or becoming a more well-rounded person. It's about signaling. The benefits of going to college aren't skill or knowledge-related, they're entirely about showing employers that you are a minimally viable candidate for their HR people to look at your application.

It's doubtful that Elon Musk gained some special set of knowledge and skills by attending Penn — but he might have gained a signal that made it easier for him to access the groups he needed to access. The professors at elite schools don't have access to some unique set of human knowledge or pedagogical techniques that makes it that their graduates are more likely to earn more over their careers than people who went to elite schools. The facilities don't magically make elite students earn more when they are 35.

(In fact, if we are looking at teaching and pedagogy, instructors at elite research universities are probably **worse** than instructors at private, liberal arts colleges. A prof at a top tier school must work on grant applications, papers for conferences and journals, do research constantly — teaching is a side-project, if that.)

The idea that grads should be grateful for some kind of human capital that the schools enabled them to develop simply isn't a good idea. Hard working, intelligent, ambitious people will gain the knowledge and skills they need for their careers wherever they are — there's nothing unique about college in endowing human capital.

Grateful For The Signal?

Okay, so the graduates don't need to be grateful for the schools giving them some kind of human capital, but what about the signal? Surely, Elon Musk's Wharton degree helped him get a job that led him to X.com and PayPal, right? Surely going to an elite institution will help your overall earnings in your lifetime, right?

It's hard to say about specific cases like Musk and others, but when we look at the earnings of people with similar backgrounds who do and do not go to elite institutions, we find that the results are essentially the same.[xxvii] It doesn't matter what the institution the person went to was, their earnings would have been just the same if they went to a less-elite institution.

So, the difference between the elite and non-elite signal is essentially negligible for high-achieving students. What can explain so many high-earners going to such few schools?

Path Dependency

One possible answer is that these schools create a sense of path dependency that drive graduates to specific fields with disproportionately high salaries (usually also with other costs associated).

Take my own school, the University of Pennsylvania, for example. Every year, more than half of all graduates go to consulting or banking jobs. Others go to graduate school, professional school, work for the government, or go to Teach For America. Is it possible that these are the desired career paths of all of these students? Possibly. But what is also likely is that graduates feel like they have to go to high-status careers in high-status locations to justify their time at an expensive, elite school. In my own time there, I heard people refer to doing work outside of these fields as "a waste of an Ivy League degree," or "something you could get with a degree from anywhere." I witnessed young people who matriculated as freshmen with the desire to go into science, art, entrepreneurship, and other fields and slowly become focused on landing a high status internship with a consulting firm or the federal government.

This is path dependency. There are different cultural and social factors that go into the decision to follow a certain track from your school. There are different paths for different schools. At Northeastern elite schools, the pressure is on to go into consulting or banking. At schools like Stanford and Michigan, the pressure is on to go work at massive tech companies. At other schools, the pressure sits for law school, teaching, working for the government, or other traditional paths.

Bill Deresiewicz talks about his own experience watching this happen in his book *Excellent Sheep*. A Yale professor,

Deresiewicz watches students who come in excited to learn about English slowly turn to a myopic focus on a career track they don't want to follow. Andrew Yang, of Venture for America, recounts a similar path during his time at Brown in his book *Smart People Should Build Things*. In *Zero to One*, Peter Thiel calls higher education "the place where people who had big plans in high school get stuck in fierce rivalries with equally smart peers over conventional careers like management consulting and investment banking."

It is possible these schools actually make people want to pursue high-salaried jobs, but at what cost to the individuals themselves?

Obvious Selection Bias

The above referenced US news article makes obvious the most likely thing operating in the background here — ambitious, hard-working, intelligent young people will be successful no matter where they go to school. Elite schools just tend to attract more of them. There's a selection bias for elite schools — the types of people who apply to them and get in are people who are likely to be successful no matter where they went to college or what path they pursue in life. This helps schools keep up the facade that they are the ones creating successful people and helps these young people stay focused on meeting certain expectations.

Meanwhile, there are more people who aren't as hard-working, ambitious, or intelligent at less-exclusive schools. This doesn't mean that these schools make people less-successful, it just means that the average student attending them was already less likely to succeed later in life.

The same goes for the college dropout, too. There are some insanely successful college dropouts who left because they felt dissatisfied with school, had better opportunities presented to them, or felt they could provide themselves with same or better opportunities for a fraction of the price. Then there are those who dropped out because they would rather eat cheetos all day. There are simply more people in the latter category. That doesn't mean that dropping out makes you want to sit around and eat cheetos every day.

In the end, the biggest contributing factor to success for a (non-) graduate isn't where they want to college but their ability to work hard, be ambitious, and live out the life that they design for themselves.

IT'S TIME WE ADMIT THE DEGREE IS SPECULATION, NOT INVESTMENT

One of the most popular tropes among career advisors, guidance counselors, school officials, and college recruiters today is that going to college is an *investment*. As more and more options for work experience and education outside of the higher education cartel crop up, those pushing the college option on young people are forced to fall back on telling the young that, though it may look costly now, it will pay off in the future. Like their Housing Crisis predecessors, they urge young people to take on the seemingly-unimaginable cost with some statistics and graphics showing that, in the recent past, a college degree pays for itself over a lifetime.

It's time that we admit that this isn't the case.

The "it's an investment!" strategy of sending young people to universities is one of the last options available to those urging people to take on this stodgy, quickly-outdated, and inefficient way to build the life that they want. If anything, this idea that it will pay off in the long run is **mere speculation, not investment.**

Let's take a look at what I mean.

In the investing world, making speculations is contrasted with making intelligent investments. Investments tend to have a safety of principle and an adequate minimum return. A speculation is something that doesn't provide this.

All investment requires an element of risk — this doesn't mean that a speculation is simply a risky investment. It's an investment that doesn't give you reason to believe that you'll actually preserve your principle (the money you initially put in) and give you a return (get you the money that you want).

Stop Citing Those ROI Studies

Here's where the college recruiter/advocate interjects, telling me that on my own definition, college is a *great* investment. "Just look at the ROI rankings put out by Payscale and Forbes and US News! They say that the data clearly point to a positive ROI!"

But this is misleading.[xxviii]

This assumes that the graduate is a mere lottery ticket and the aggregate of all the attendees at their school. This includes comparing a petroleum engineer to a philosophy major to a Gender Studies major to a business student. At best, this just tells us more about the selection bias in these schools.

(In short, **these schools take people who would probably be successful anyways and then claim credit for their success**. It's a great recruiting and fundraising tactic, really.)

To rely on this data is to be too quick to declare that the degree is an investment with a minimum ROI. A better study would be to take a large sample who got into the same university (status really doesn't matter),[xxix] with the same SAT scores and aptitudes, and follow them over the course of their careers as

217

half drop out and half completes the degree. You would also have to control for elements like where they moved, family structure, background, and more.

If this sounds ridiculous, it's because it is. There are so many other factors that go into determining the success or failure of a young person over the span of their careers that to turn it on one issue is ludicrous.

But let us assume that the college factor is the overriding, major contributing factor to one's career. Maybe ROI isn't the best factor. What about attempting to get the job?

If Job Is What Matters, The Degree Is Probably Speculation

Most young people go to college to get a job, not to get an education or to open themselves up to new and interesting viewpoints. If you think this sounds cynical, follow a simple thought experiment next time you meet a group of college students.

Ask them if they would still pay whatever they (or somebody else) are paying for their degree if, when they graduated, they stood no better chance at employment (or even a worse chance!) than when they started. If they're being honest with you, most would tell you no, they would not still go.

While a good job should be related to financial gains, it's not always a direct correlation, so maybe a better determiner of return is whether or not graduates land in jobs that require degrees.

If that's the case, then the data are sketchy.

In 2013, only 27% of college grads landed a job in a field related to their major. But around 60% landed a job requiring a degree.

You could attribute this percentage to a slow recovery, assuming it would increase year-over-year as job prospects improve across the economy as a whole.

You'd be wrong.

In 2014, only 51% of college graduates landed jobs that required degrees, down nearly 10% from the year before. [xxx]

It's too early to really say what 2015 yields for college graduates, but this trend isn't surprising to me. I spend most of my time talking to employers and scouring careers sites, looking for trends and trying to get ahead of the pack so that I can provide the best education-training experience possible. One of the major trends I noticed, even among traditionally stodgy industries like accounting, consulting, and advertising, is that employers care more about what you can do than about what you claim than ever before. The rise in "degree or equivalent work experience" is stronger than ever. The rise of the Internet and of personal digital brands makes it much easier for an employer to verify claims about whether or not a person knows something. This means more companies can move away from the credential requirement as a filtering mechanism and instead switch over to simply googling a candidate, looking up their LinkedIn, or being provided with a professional portfolio.

Of course, if your mission is to land a job in an industry protected by legal degree requirements, like accounting, medicine, or law, then the undergraduate degree is a great investment. If your goal is to land a job in general, then you're probably speculating.

You're Not A Retirement Account

If you want something safe that will yield a decent ROI in the investment world, something like a Vanguard or a Fidelity ETF account is what most people use. It's highly diversified between different kinds of stocks and with some federal and municipal bonds. It won't make you rich, but it should give you more money than with which you started.

You're not a retirement account, though.

You can't diversify yourself between a half-dozen different options in career, education, schooling, credentialing, and skills.

In fact, the pursuit of college, especially elite college, dilutes your ability to valuably invest in yourself.

While you should be focusing on the things that you know and that you know well, the things that you can do well, and the things that you enjoy the most, you spend your most formative years diversifying your skills and experience portfolio to the point that you can't yield all that much more than if you just stayed home and didn't really do anything.

This is how investing for a big payoff works, too. Warren Buffett invests in things that he knows and things that he knows *well*. All of the best investors make a smaller number of higher-knowledge investments. Thiel urges against diversification if you want to really excel, both in investing and in yourself.

Know What You Want

The problem with education and schooling is the same as the problem with too many wannabe investors today — people don't know what they want. They go in with a general lofty goal like, "get a good job," or "buy a house," or "get rich," without putting actual parameters on these goals. What is a good job? Why do you want the house? How rich? When? Why? How?

It's a continuation of what Thiel calls "indefinite optimism." People work towards general goals and general needs for "better," but don't actually know what paths make up this "better."

In education and schooling this means we are just constantly moving from one goalpost to the next, rarely asking what the end goal is and why we are following that path. We want to go to a good high school and get good grades so that we can get into a good college so that we can go to a good graduate school so that we can land a good job so that we can...what?

> "Indefinite attitudes to the future explain what's most dysfunctional in our world today. Process trumps substance: when people lack concrete plans to carry out, they use formal rules to assemble a portfolio of various options. This describes Americans today. In middle school, we're encouraged to start hoarding "extracurricular activities." In high school, ambitious students compete even harder to appear omnicompetent. By the time a student gets to college, he's spent a decade curating a bewilderingly diverse résumé to prepare for a completely unknowable future. Come what may, he's ready—for nothing in particular."
> — Peter Thiel, Zero to One

Many students attend college to get a good job without asking why they are going in the first place, what kind of job they want to have, what kind of life they want to live, and what they want to make of themselves. They think in general terms. This applies to their spending and saving habits once they get out of college. Why should they save now? The money has always been there for them, they can get loans to go to college, buy a house, get a car, etc.

This leads people to speculate not only with their educations but with their careers, too. Speculating with your career leads to speculating with your family life, your hobbies, your friends, and generally leads to an indefinite, unstable future.

Consider The Alternatives

When you don't know what you want from your life or career, going to college quickly jumps from being an investment to being a speculation. Even good colleges can't make up for that fact.

Most studies and talks of whether or not degrees are worth the time and money assume the alternative is sitting around being a stoner on the couch and eating doritos. This doesn't have to be the case, though. If you spend this time constructively, building your human and social capital, engaging with ideas and actually seeking an education (contra just a credential), then you can come out making much more with this time than your peers.

For more high-achieving young people today, knowing what they want and building a path to get there will prove to be a much stronger investment than blowing four years on an indefinite shot at "a good job."

REQUIRE A DEGREE AT YOUR OWN RISK

Let's say you are an employer of a fast-paced, growing, interesting small-to-medium sized organization. Every person you hire has a huge impact on your organization, and they can make or break the team with which they are placed. You put a lot of effort and resources into guaranteeing that those you hire are the right culture, skills, and interest-fits for your organization. One fluke and you have to fire them quickly or watch the disproportionate problems they may bring with them.

You put an opening online and wait for applications and resumes to come in. You sift through these trying to find the right candidates. Hypothetically, you should have some sort of mechanism to weed out the serious candidates from the non-serious candidates. For many organizations, this is what the degree requirement is supposed to do. You put "A BA is required to apply for this position," on the listing, hoping that will help you solve your problems. It may, to a certain extent. Some of the people just churning resumes out to companies after just completing high school and doing little more for a few years may be weeded out. "Aha! This will surely signal to me the serious candidates!"

But think about *your own* time in college. Think of how, even if you went to an elite university, there would be days when more than a few students would show up hungover for class, if they showed up at all. Most students were primarily concerned with what social activities were happening that weekend — studies were an afterthought. Even at liberal arts colleges focused on teaching, many professors hadn't changed their curricula in years, and treat their students like children (if not openly, then with other professors or on social media).

Your own BA is worth just as much as the kid who showed up drunk to class twice, nearly failed into econ, and just did the bare minimum to get on by. It signals to employers that you are a minimally acceptable candidate *at his level*, not that he is at yours.

All those applications going across your desk now are at least at that level. Who are you leaving out?

You're excluding the entrepreneurial young person who dropped out of college at 20 to go found his own company, or to get experience — maybe even in the field you are hiring for — in the workplace rather than in the classroom. You are excluding the person who is a creative problem solver, who has learned-by-doing, and who has thought quickly on their feet. You may even be excluding one of your very own employees who wants to come on in a fuller capacity. In short, you are excluding exactly whom you are trying to hire.

"Okay, maybe I am excluding that person, but the nobodies that I am excluding surely outnumber him."

Maybe. And if there were no other way to differentiate this person from those people, that would be a very good reason to require the I-showed-up-for-four-years-and-was-minimally-acceptable signal (i.e., the degree). The good news is, with the advent of the Internet, with sites like LinkedIn, WordPress, a digital track record, and open-sourced learning, you can check these people out very quickly. Even better news: you don't need to do that much work.

Let's imagine you have a candidate apply for the position you are hiring for. She has more experience than any other candidate, has golden references, and has a track-record of creating value in the workplace. She's your ideal candidate. Except she never went to college.

What do you gain from excluding her? What do you gain from hiring the next-best candidate — who may be considerably worse — who just happens to have a degree?

If you're a large company that looks to bring people on, groom them, make them senior employees over time, and put lots of resources into them, you probably *do* want somebody who can signal that they can put up with arbitrary rules and patterns for four years over the person who signals they may not.

But if you're a company that values entrepreneurialism, risk-taking, and the ability to take ownership for one's actions, then a lack of a BA should be a *good* sign, if anything. It could show this person is willing to take ownership over what they do, their life, and their ability to create in the world.

Being a credentialist (requiring a degree to apply for a position) only hurts one person and group at the end of the day: you and your company. Be a credentialist at your own risk. You don't know who you are excluding.

ERNST & YOUNG DOESN'T REQUIRE DEGREES — WHY DO YOU?

Earlier this year, Ernst and Young, one of the biggest professional services firms in the world, dropped a bombshell that they would no longer be requiring college degrees for candidates applying to join their teams. In a statement, EY announced:[xxxi]

> *[We] found no evidence to conclude that previous success in higher education correlated with future success in subsequent professional qualifications undertaken.*

And while EY did not say that they wouldn't be considering the degree *at all* for candidates, they did say that it will no longer be taken into account for getting one's foot through the door. Still a bombshell, considering that most people admit that while their degree was not particularly useful in adding human capital, it was helpful for them to get their foot through the door.

Instead, EY will be turning to more accurate measurements of future success, like skills tests, aptitude tests, and looking at what a candidate has actually accomplished in the past (versus through which hoops a degree says they jumped).

This is surprising because Ernst & Young isn't exactly the shining beacon of "drop-out-of-college-and-go-found-a-startup" sexiness that has taken the world by storm in the past few years. It's exactly the kind of company that Peter Thiel describes in *Zero to One* as not really creating anything new, and instead "shuffling around existing resources" through its work.

If one of the world's largest, most established, and stodgiest companies realizes that making a blunt degree requirement shuts you off to the very best talent and that there are better mechanisms for finding top talent out there in the 21st century, then you have to sit back and ask yourself the same question EY did:

WHY ARE YOU REQUIRING A DEGREE?

Most people doing hiring aren't exactly sure *why* they require a degree, just that they do. They sit back, imagine their ideal candidate, draw up a list of experiences and skills, and just tack the degree on to the end as an afterthought. The ideal candidate probably has a degree, but **it isn't the degree that makes the person the ideal candidate.**

This means that the ideal candidate might be out there without the degree — but if we just took a pool of young people and looked at those with and those without degrees, our candidate is more likely to be in the former pool. In an age when work can be verified with a simple Google search and when skills can be verified with an online quiz, this is a suboptimal recruiting tactic.

This is an odd realization to have, but the curious history of the degree as a signal of success and of aptitude gives us an idea of why it is that we got ourselves here.

The Curious History Of Degrees

The undergraduate degree requirement was once an intuitive filter for finding good talent, but more and more hiring managers and entrepreneurs are realizing this isn't the case. At one time, a university was one of the only places you could go to receive any kind of education outside of K-12 — and, unless you were a master autodidact, one of the few hopes for continuing education. For companies, this meant that going to the universities would yield them the best young people to come work for them.

An attempt to set candidates apart by IQ ends in a trip to the US Supreme Court with Griggs v. Duke Power Co., making it that employers have to rely on universities to filter candidates out by relative intelligence. This SCOTUS ruling is one of the biggest boons to the success of the university cartel in the 20th century.

As young people realized that the degree was the ticket to a steady middle class job, more went to college. More colleges opened their doors to even more students, for-profit colleges popped up to get on the bandwagon, and the government subsidized these schools by the dozens through the GI bill, grants, student loans, and more.

At this point, companies are pretty much forced to require degrees (remember, this is in the pre-Internet era still), lest the HR manager have to rifle through hundreds of applications for one post. After all, if everybody who is slightly below-average and better has a degree, then you might as well as filter those who don't, right?

As more people came out of colleges, the relative power of the undergraduate degree got weaker. Employers now must rifle through just as many applications as before the degree requirement became standard, but now having a BA doesn't really signal anything much to them. It tells them, "oh, you can sit in a classroom and do what you are told for four years and pay your life savings for it!"

The mass popularization of the degree — led by individuals hoping to set themselves apart from the pack — ultimately makes all those who are trying to set themselves apart look the same. It weakens the hiring power of employers and it weakens relative prospects of the youth (who could have spent the time and money wasted on the degree on ventures more likely to really set themselves apart).

Even worse for the power of the degree, more high-achieving young people are passing on it today than ever before. As the Internet lowers costs for launching projects, joining fellowships, cofounding companies, and learning without the classroom, employers requiring degrees are just shutting themselves off to the very best talent.

> *Not long ago dropping out of school to start a company was considered risky. For this generation, it is a badge of honor, evidence of ambition and focus.*
> *— Wall Street Journal, June 5, 2015*[xxxii]

Employers are now forced to make a decision: either require *more* credentials from entry level candidates to set themselves apart (I saw an unpaid internship in Long Island this summer that required a Master's degree!), or **to use a better signal — what you know and what you've done**. The latter is what Ernst & Young did — why haven't you?

The New Better Signal

The revolution in higher education is happening all around us and nobody notices. It isn't driven by MOOCs or by more online courses or apps. It's not driven by MIT or Yale making their courses open and available to all. It's driven by tools like Google, LinkedIn, WordPress, Github, and the Internet as a whole. **For the first time in history, any candidate can build a better signal.**

Employers now have a much less costly way to verify whether or not a candidate has done what they say they have done and knows what they say they know. A quick Google search can find projects the candidate developed, stories they wrote, and features about them. A well-catered LinkedIn profile works as more than just a resume — it's a professional portfolio that signals so much more competence than "B.A., Class of 2011" on an application does. Personal sites and blogs allow candidates to treat themselves as brands and can show off both the knowledge and the experience of a candidate with ease.

Aptitude tests can now be administered remotely through the Internet, lowering the costs for employers to test candidates on what they claim to know. The skills and knowledge necessary to ace these exams no longer sits only in the dusty libraries of universities, but at the fingertips of every person with a smartphone.

"How can this be implemented in hiring practices? A BA requirement is an easy tweak in an online application, do you really expect every hiring manager to Google every candidate?"

Absolutely not. But just as a BA requirement is an easy tweak in an application, adding a just-as-significant area for a portfolio, LinkedIn, or personal site is also easy. Removing the BA requirement so candidates can get past the filter and show off their better signals is the best step that companies can take to open themselves up to the best young talent out there. These are the young people who are focused and driven to create the best experiences for themselves possible, not just wait passively for them to arrive.

You have nothing to lose and everything to gain by considering these young people building a better signal.

DEGREE INFLATION IS OUT OF CONTROL - HERE'S HOW TO FIX THAT

I had coffee with a friend of mine the other day who recently graduated from college. After the parties and the Facebook posts from aunts and uncles saying, "I'm so proud of you, congratulations!!!" he continued his long hunt for a job. He was first surprised and then merely discouraged to hear at every turn that employers weren't interested in hiring him.

He was interested in working for a major airline in a summer internship only to be told no because they wanted a Master's degree for the internship. It was unpaid.

Flustered and discouraged, he admitted to me that,

It seems like my college degree is the new high school diploma.

He may sound entitled, but the thing is, **he's right**. The relative value of a degree for employers means less today than ever before.

The New High School Diploma

At one time, employers could look at a college degree as a signal that a candidate not only had a great work ethic and a strong sense of follow-through but that they were cut from a different cloth from most average or above-average young people. It signaled something unique about the candidate and made it that they were somebody in whom it would make sense to invest.

As time went on and more people saw that having a college degree was strongly correlated with moving into the middle class, more and more people strived to go to college. Government loan and grant programs subsidized more students, producing more college graduates.

On the face of it, this could mean that there are more qualified workers for the workforce. More people with a greater level of skills, with more follow-through, and with more work ethic than ever should be joining the workforce.

Right?

Wrong.

More Degrees, Fewer Skills

Despite more people achieving the height of Baby Boomer-success, there's a real and serious skills gap for employers trying to fill positions. Many college graduates come armed with some loose understanding of theory but few skills and little work experience to put to use. According to the Harvard Business Review:

> *Last year, 35% of 38,000 employers reported difficulty filling jobs due to lack of available talent, in the U.S., 39% of employers did.* [xxxiii]

Despite sending more people to college, fewer graduates are equipped to deal with the changing technologies and strategies of the workforce. The HBR goes on to note that the skills lacking in recent graduates are those with which schools cannot by their nature equip people:

> *[T]here are not major shortages of workers with basic reading and math skills or of workers with engineering and technical training; if anything, too many workers may be overeducated.*

So where do we go from here? How can we address the skills gap and address education at the same time?

Two Paths Forward

The relative value of the degree ended up meaning less to an employer as more candidates came to the table with them. Instead of the college graduate being an extraordinary young person standing apart from the pack, he became a minimally viable candidate who would need yet another way of differentiating himself.

Inflation, Inflation, Inflation

HR departments and hiring managers, looking for the quickest, most efficient ways to select for the best-equipped candidates continued to use the blunt tool of the degree to sort candidates out. Following the logic that got us to a point of worthless college degrees, some just upped the ante and started requiring more degrees for positions that couldn't conceivably need one (like the unpaid internship I mention above).

The Washington Post noted last year:

> *[A] wide range of jobs — in management, administration, sales and other fields — are undergoing "upcredentialing," or degree inflation. As examples, just 25 percent of people employed as insurance clerks have a BA, but twice that percentage of insurance-clerk job ads require one. Among executive secretaries and executive assistants, 19 percent of job-holders have degrees, but 65 percent of job postings mandate them.* [xxxiv]

If we want to require degrees for even the most basic entry-level jobs, this is one way of approaching things. Companies with massive hiring departments and little creativity for finding new candidates are already requiring BAs for many unpaid internships. Some even extend this to graduate students, figuring that the most skilled candidates might as well have the highest number of credentials.

But do we really want to require that somebody spend a third of his life in school, apart from the market and the workforce and apart from learning real-world skills before we are willing to hire him? Do we really think that requiring more and more credentials is the best way to foster a highly-skilled and ambitious generation that is capable of the creative thinking and problem solving necessary for 21st century success? If this track of degree inflation continues, you will need a PhD in cleaning studies to get a job as janitorial intern. (We're not far from this -- there are more janitors in the US today with chemistry degrees than there are chemists.)

Build A Better Signal

We can continue down this path of massive degree inflation and wait for what kinds of talent it reaps, or **we can take a different path.**

The degree worked as a decent blunt tool for those doing hiring when the cost of finding out whether or not a candidate knew their stuff was so incredibly high. You could never administer an IQ test, an aptitude test, a work assignment, and call all the former employers of a given candidate in a timely and cost-efficient manner.

But a massive technological innovation over the past two decades has made it easier for companies to actually verify talent and find the best without relying on the blunt tool that is the degree. **The Internet came along and people could verify their skills and their experience in one simple place.** Platforms like LinkedIn, where you are reading this right now, aren't merely places to put a digital resume and to send connection requests -- they're repositories of verified talent, experience, and skills the likes of which the world has never seen before.

A quick example:

I had a phone conversation with a young man this morning who connected with me on LinkedIn. Before our call, I Googled his name and poked around his profile here to learn a little more about him. In those 5 minutes I learned so much more about his ability to think critically and analytically, write well, execute on projects, and find creative solutions than I would have if I had seen "B.A., Example University" on a job application.

His degree -- or lack thereof -- was a complete and total afterthought.

If you had told somebody to "build a better signal to employers than a college degree" before the Internet, a select few extremely high-caliber candidates could do that, but most couldn't because they would have no way of showing off that signal with ease in an application. With the Internet and platforms like LinkedIn, Wordpress, Squarespace, and About.me, this is now possible. Now any candidate who is reasonably skilled, ambitious, and competent can build a better signal.

And we are all much better off for it.

This can be done a variety of ways: building independent projects, freelancing, taking up a job with an entrepreneur and building their digital brand out, and so much more. What is important is that there are people out there who can communicate the value they create outside of the schooled context. **Requiring higher levels of schooling just to get an entry level job only hurts employers by depriving themselves of this talent.**

So what will it be? Will we continue down the path of degree inflation to the point where we'll need degrees for welders and garbage collectors and janitors? **Or will we throw off this antiquated model and accept the fact that some of the most high-caliber candidates can build a better signal?**

WHERE ARE ALL OF THE YOUNG ENTREPRENEURS?

There's a popular trope right now that a ton of young people are founders and entrepreneurs. Thanks to a handful of young founders with a disproportionate impact (aka Mark Zuckerberg) and cultural figures like HBO's *Silicon Valley*, you can easily trick yourself into believing that entrepreneurship is all the craze among young people. Hacker meetups, entrepreneurship clubs and majors on college campuses, and the sudden growth of incubators and accelerator programs can present some sexy fodder for this case.

But this is all misleading. Entrepreneurship among young people is actually relatively *uncommon*. Relatively few young people today own stock in a private company — and a good chunk of those who do likely aren't entrepreneurs anyway, but rather work for companies who issue equity to their employees.

According to the *Wall Street Journal* (behind a paywall, google the title to gain access to the article), the percentage of young Americans who are entrepreneurs dipped to less than 4% in 2015:

> *Roughly 3.6% of households headed by adults younger than 30 owned stakes in private companies, according to an analysis by The Wall Street Journal of recently released Federal Reserve data from 2013. That compares with 10.6% in 1989—when the central bank*

began collecting standard data on Americans' incomes and net worth—and 6.1% in 2010. [xxxv]

The *Journal* offers a couple of hypotheses as to what is behind the dip in entrepreneurship among young people, including stiffer competition in the age of the Internet, lower savings rates among young people in the aftermath of the recession, a decreased appetite for risk, and changes in bank lending policies. These all are possible contributing factors, but I suspect that formal institutions play a larger role in the decline in business ownership.

Between local, state, and federal regulations placed on everything from who is allowed to braid hair to who can tell you what color to paint a wall and where to place a door and a schooling culture and system that encourages young people to waste away the first 22-30 years of their lives away from the market, the systems placed upon young people today create a climate extremely hostile to entrepreneurship and economic growth.

Regulated To Economic Death

Americans today are the most regulated and taxed in the country's history. While some tax rates have dropped in recent years, they've been offset by increases elsewhere and the unprecedented and massive growth in the bureaucracy. It's harder today to simply start a business because of the number of regulations with which one must comply. It was once possible to start a business whenever you realized you were on to something that solved problems for people and for which they would pay you, but the immense regulation of small businesses today makes the barrier to entry so much higher that plucky young upstarts are much less likely to be able to get off the ground.

A few decades ago, Tina may have started a small salon out of her basement when she realized that she had a knack for designing nice and fun haircuts for her friends and family and also realized that this could earn her some extra money for her kids. She'd clear some space away in the basement, put up a sign advertising her service, and even have her nephew man the front desk as business picked up. Not so today. Today, she'd have to pass a number of boards and certifying examinations saying that she is qualified to provide this service (never mind if customers thought she was qualified — it was her competitors who would judge her boards and exams), get a commercial license from her local government, incorporate as a business, get a federal EIN for tax purposes, buy a regulation-friendly sign, and hire staff at a much higher price than her nephew was willing to do the work. And that's just to get off the ground and get started.

Is it any wonder that Tina doesn't go into business today?

Taxing Investment

One of the most nefarious taxation schemes to small business and entrepreneurial growth is the capital gains tax. Used in this election cycle to refer to taxes on "hedge fund managers" (a boogeyman of choice in Election 2016), the capital gains tax is, simply put, the tax on gains from investments. This applies to all sorts of investments, not just millions of dollars made from trading in some dark room like in *The Wolf of Wall Street*. If you flip a house, you have to pay a capital gains tax. If you invest in commodities (i.e., oil, gold, silver, sugar, copper), you have to pay a capital gains tax. If you start a business that issues dividends, you have to pay a capital gains tax.

Most investments (including launching a small business) come with a certain level of risk and are only made if the would-be investor can expect a minimal growth on the payout. If they know that half of their profits are going to be taxed away by the feds and the state government, many people will decide to forego the investment in the first place. Why work twice as hard at creating a profitable business so that you can keep just as much (if not less!) than a waged job would provide?

I have a good friend who flipped a house when he was 16 years old. He and a few friends put all the money they had saved up together to buy an old house. With a loan from the bank, they owned the house and renovated it heavily. They ended up selling it for a 3x ROI. By the time the state and federal taxes were through, they each received a few thousand dollars over their initial investment. At that point, *it would have been wiser to go work at McDonald's for a year* rather than work on the house.

If you have to pay an income tax and a capital gains tax on everything that you worked so hard to build as a small businessperson, what incentive remains to start in the first place? Sure, there are stories about being the one in charge of your work and how good that feels, but you have to pay your bills at the end of the day. Young people know this too well after years of little-to-no financial education and then seeing the FICA taxes on their paychecks the first few times.

Occupational Licensure & Cost of Working

It's not uncommon to have to pass tests in certain states in order to do your trade. If you're a doctor or an airline pilot, this might make intuitive sense. But what about a florist? Or a hair braider? An interior designer?

Defenders of occupational licensure will usually find fringe cases where being "properly qualified" to do a job would have supposedly prevented a negative outcome or will point to how hard they had to work to get to where they are today, but these licenses are almost always just some kind of rent-seeking by firms currently in the market trying to keep out potential competitors. Most of these boards and exams are designed and/or judged by existing firms (would-be competitors) and can be extremely costly.

Going back to our hairdresser, Tina, she would have to pass her state qualifications before she can dress hair for people. If she wanted to do cutting at her shop, there's a good chance she'd have to pass another set of tests and requirements before she can offer that radical service. This means she'll have to find the time to go to classes, the money to pay for classes and offset the cost of not working while taking classes, and hope that she passes the examination at the end of the classes.

She may, then, be forced to join a union and pay union dues on top of everything else.

Growing Your Business

Let's say you're a young person who has decided to bear the brunt of the capital gains tax on top of an income tax, the brunt of the regulations declaring how you can and cannot make your living, and even the brunt of any occupational licensure, now it's time to build your business. After operating for a few months, you realize you could use an extra set of hands around your studio to help organize and clean up. You have a friend who is willing to do it in his spare time for a little gas money on the side.

Not so fast! This gas money doesn't cover the minimum wage that your friend is entitled to by law. If you fail to pay him this and the department of labor finds out, you'll be slapped with fines making business impossible for a firm of your size.

So you decide to pay him a minimum wage. Your margins continue to shrink but you could use the extra hands around. As you grow, you could use a second specialist to join you. You have to cut your friend in order to pay for the specialist. The combined cost wasn't worth the marginal addition in value.

It's time to open a second location. Hooray! You've been impressive in your growth and can reinvest some of your profits into a new location. You'll employ more people, serve more happy customers, and all the while grow as a business.

You want to move into the next county over where there is a larger customer base. You find the property, have an agent hired, and are ready to go when you look into the regulations. This new county requires a number of additional licenses to do business and levies a county tax on "corporations." The voters likely thought this meant some company that has offices all over the world and employs people in suits to eat babies — but it turns out that your business is, too, a corporation. You pull back your plans for expansion and settle on staying in your county.

Tech: A Free Domain?

The heavy regulations and taxes placed on trade-based and investment-based businesses might explain why more young people are interested in launching tech companies instead of these traditional operations. Government regulators are notoriously slow to figuring out new technologies (I still have to pay my municipal sewage bill by mail) and the decentralized, low-cost nature of the Internet makes it harder to levy regulations on firms based there instead of a brick-and-mortar location. It should be no surprise, then, that this area is more prone to seeing startups than elsewhere. The regulations levied on a digital marketing firm are fewer than those of a traditional ad agency or for a logistics app instead of a taxi service. Software engineering is a totally new trade compared to construction, and the forces at play stifling construction have yet to develop for software engineering.

As government regulators and rent-seekers learn the ropes of Internet-based firms and as their tracking technologies improve, expect to see it become much harder to create a tech-based product and company.

Drowning in Debt

Legal and regulatory barriers to entry likely discourage a good number of would-be entrepreneurs who are lucky enough to get that far in the planning process. Unfortunately, for more and more young Americans, debt from student loans takes a higher priority than entrepreneurial planning.

Increasing costs of college combined with easy-money from government-backed agencies and banks have made it that around 71% of graduates in 2015 had student loans (up from 64% in 2005 and up from < 50% 20 years ago). The average graduate in 2015 has more than $35,000 in student loan debt — meaning that half of the grads have more than this.[xxxvi] And the trends are just pointing to these numbers increasing.

Launching a risky venture with no guarantee of return on investment is hard enough without debt — it's nearly impossible when you have hundreds of dollars of student loans to pay back every month. Even if you can get the loans deferred, you still have to worry about whether or not you'll get to the income levels needed to pay it off in the future.

The Philadelphia Fed reported a strong negative correlation between business formation for businesses with one to four employees and student loan debt.[xxxvii] Similarly, areas with a high amount of student loan debt also see the smallest growth in small businesses.[xxxviii]

Most small businesses are funded with personal debt in the form of small loans from banks and acquaintances and credit card debt, not huge venture capital pushes as depicted in recent media. Crushing student loan debt makes it harder to manage a $10,000 line of credit on a credit card or a loan from a bank.

But if we recall the WSJ report showing the decline in business ownership between 1989 and 2015, we'll see that the biggest dip happened *before* the recent spike in outstanding student debt. The growth in lifetime-crushing student debt likely contributes heavily to the decline in the past 15 years, but the fact that a large dip happened before this period might indicate that **the problem isn't that fewer people can't start businesses** but rather that **people don't want to start businesses.**[xxxix]

Young people are more likely to take a "safe" and "stable" job than own a business, recent data indicate.[xl] There are a variety of additional factors that influence this, but one of the largest is the level at which young people are schooled. The current generation of recent graduates and young professionals is more schooled than any generation before them. Despite this, a growing skill gap and discontentment with work and personal life plagues them.[xli][xlii]

Over-schooled and Over-coddled: Risk

The preference of a "safe" and "stable" job (assuming there is such a thing) over owning a business is likely a consequence of being more risk averse than prior generations.[xliii][xliv] Young people today grew up in a weird paradoxical world of being rewarded for everything and being instilled with an intense fear of failure.

Being told that you deserve a reward just for participating creates an odd sense of resentment to even trying in most children. Children are smart enough to know when they are being talked down to, and adults giving them awards for not doing their best feels patronizing, even to a six year old. Why work harder if it is just going to result in the same kind of reward? Why try to get somebody to praise you if they'll do it when you fail anyway?

As children grow older and move into the competitive middle school and high school environments, failure takes on a new tone. Failing at school — which takes up the vast majority of a young adult's life from 6 AM – 5 PM most days for the first 18 years — amounts to failing at much of life. Failing an exam or a class translated into failing out of the top echelon of the schooling world — you wouldn't amount to much in school, wouldn't get into a university of your choice, wouldn't get the job you wanted, and would be relegated to an unhappy existence for the rest of your life. Many, many schoolchildren would rather cheat on exams and risk being caught than risk failing the exam outright.

Even in the extra-curricular world, young adults are overworked and overscheduled. Between competition from peers and pressure from parents, a young person competing in anything from soccer to quiz bowl can't afford to fail. The cost of being found out as a cheater or as a flake are lower than the perceived costs of failure.

A healthy level of risk-tolerance is necessary for success in business. Even traditional businesses have to take risks in taking out loans, trying out new products, and offering services in the community. Most successful entrepreneurs are courageous — a trait that school and a coddling parental generation can beat out of young people.

Over-Schooled: Degree Inflation

Most business owners held some kind of other job before launching their business. If they're working in the startup world and are offering a new and unique service, chances are even higher that they worked for years in a specialized field before launching their product or service. The spike in degree inflation has made it harder to enter the workforce at a younger age. Jobs that had no or minimal credentialing requirements just a few years ago now require a BA or a graduate degree. It's not uncommon to find internships that require a graduate degree.

Getting your foot in the door and gaining experience as a young person is harder than ever. For many entrepreneurs, this experience at another firm was integral to their own venture. This means that would-be entrepreneurs find themselves putting off ventures for years while they complete the formal education requirements to gain the experience they feel is necessary before launching.

Add in the additional factor of life happening and more would-be entrepreneurs drop from the pool. Having 5 years of experience might have made you 27 before out-of-control degree inflation, but today it very well may make you 33 because you had to spend a few years working internships and getting a graduate degree to get that entry level job. Now you have a wife, a baby, a mortgage, and some debt from school, adding more constraints on the flexibility you need to launch a company. You decide to stay at your old job for your family and keep on your way.

Over-Schooled: Schooled Minds

One final factor that I suspect contributes to the decline in entrepreneurship is the effect that schooling has on thinking differently. Successful entrepreneurs (and successful people in general) cite thinking differently than the pack as one of the most important factors for their success. Whether it's making an investment will pay off big time or going to work somewhere that has a lot of potential for growth, these people all set themselves apart first by their thinking that allowed them to make these decisions. They then had the work ethic to carry through and execute on these ideas.

Schools are notorious for promoting conformity of thought and making people resent the idea of working hard. They promote homogeneity of thought through mandatory curricula and separating young people by age. This is no hippie-dippie, new agey bullshit, either. Think about it in terms of economic thinking.

A young person in school has a strong incentive to mold their way of thinking to that of the people around them. In class, they are rewarded for meeting and exceeding expectations on rubrics and standardized tests. Try as they may, it is nearly impossible for teachers to develop a standard curriculum that promotes difference in thought. Smart students know what their teachers want from exams and will give it to them. The cost of doing things differently is much higher than the cost of conforming to standards and expectations. If you do things differently, expect to pay the cost.

In the lunch room and in the halls, little is different. Having different opinions or lifestyle tastes earns a child or young adult the ridicule of peers and the displeasure of being an outcast.

To succeed in the schooling environment requires nearly the exact opposite as succeeding in the marketplace — an above-average work ethic is the only arguable shared trait. Schools reward conformity in thought and problem-solving. They reward conformity in tastes and desires. The kid who wants to go off and do something entirely different than his peers is shunned or at least finds it difficult to make friends. The young adult who solves problems differently than the textbook is slowed down and made to feel inferior. Having a definite focus is discouraged, especially if it does not relate directly to exams. — instead, focus on getting good grades and getting out of school to succeed.

Success as a young entrepreneur requires an element of deschooling —unlearning the bad habits built up during school. In fact, many affluent entrepreneurs *were not high-achieving students in school.*[xlv]

The Devil's In The Institutions

The factors that contribute to whether or not somebody decides to launch a business can be broken down into if they can and if they want to. Increases in taxes and government regulations — especially those on small business owners and tradespeople — combined with an immense spike in student loan debt and stricter lending policies by banks make it harder for those who want to start businesses to even get off the ground. An ever-growing schooling regime that rewards conformity of thought and heavily penalizes risk-taking creates a generation of people who don't even want to become entrepreneurs anyway.

To see the next (and current, lost) generation of business owners, value-creators, and innovators take off, freedom to experiment, fail, and the opportunity to try different things need to be reclaimed.

I suspect that this demographic factor — having parents who are entrepreneurs begets being an entrepreneur yourself — has even wider implications than the immediate children. Growing up with entrepreneurship in your household makes it seem less daunting, but so does growing up with it in your community. Fewer entrepreneur parents not only mean fewer entrepreneur children, **it means fewer entrepreneurs in general** as the profession moves further and further away from the average young person.

ENTREPRENEURSHIP IS THE SOLUTION TO HIGHER EDUCATION -- NOT MORE COLLEGE

"In order to stay competitive in the global economy, we have to make sure as many people as possible are educated to the greatest extent possible!"

"A college degree is the only way to get ahead in the 21st century!"

"Higher education must be a top priority going forward!"

These and similar tropes are popular among pundits, recruiters, higher education professionals and young people. The idea is intuitive — if the rest of the world is accelerating in its growth and advancements like the industrialized west, then it is more and more important to set yourself apart from the swaths of other young people joining the workforce with a formal education. While a basic secondary education may have gotten you by yesterday, post-secondary and graduate education is what will be necessary to set you apart tomorrow.

While intuitive, this solution gets the problem entirely wrong and will only exacerbate the talent and education crisis that employers and investors are seeing today.

The assumption behind this solution is that going to college and university is a human capital play made by young people to make them more valuable. They go to learn skills and gain knowledge that they can apply in the marketplace. Sure, along the way they may learn something about literature or art history that really makes them feel like they are becoming well-rounded, but the real assumption is that they'll learn skills that are marketable to employers and others in the "real world."

The problem is that this assumption gets the reason young people go to college entirely wrong. It assumes that they go to college as scruffy, starry eyed hunks of raw human capital yet to be molded into hard-working, skilled, ambitious people who can suddenly come out much more accelerated in their growth than when they entered.

The Degree Is A Signal, Not Much More

The real reason most young people go to college and are pushed to go to college is because they feel like they have to go if they want a job. Some, mostly in highly technical fields like engineering and accounting (even law and medicine are mostly learned at the graduate level, not undergrad), pick up skills while in school, but most go because they are told that they need a degree to get a job. It's a signaling play, not a human capital play.

You can see this with a simple thought experiment. If you went to a campus in the United States and asked a handful of students you found on campus if they would still go to college if their chances of finding a job upon graduation were unchanged, most would tell you no, they would probably not (and this is a really charitable reading of the college experience. If you removed most 18 year olds from the marketplace for four years while they picked up no concrete skills, experiences, or networks and instead fiddled away at underwater basket weaving of the pan-asian diaspora instead of working, their employability at 22 or 23 would likely be much *lower* than at 18).

They go to college because they feel like they have to. Parents, teachers, guidance counselors and other adults believe that human resources managers and recruiters won't even look at them without degrees.

The Degree Is A Poor Signal

The paradox is that this pushes more and more young people to get a degree — a tool for setting themselves apart from others — which in turn devalues the power of the signal to employers. When at one time 10 in 100 applicants for a job had a degree, now 80 in 100 do. These 70 new people in the pool look like each other and aren't any better off (and much poorer) than when they didn't have the degree.

By pushing young people to "stay competitive" in the world, we push them into a position where they have no choice but to continue on this hamster wheel. We're already seeing the perverse consequences of this push for more and more credentialing. It's not uncommon for entry-level jobs to require Master's degrees when years ago they barely required a BA. Employers have been forced to up the entry requirement to filter out a spike in otherwise-unqualified applicants with BAs.

The thing is, "staying competitive" is overrated.

Competition is for losers.

In any market, competition drives profits to zero in the long run. The labor market is no different.

If a young person today wants to set themselves apart, doing what the pack is being encouraged to do is exactly what they *shouldn't* do.

There's a better option for gaining skills, valuable experience, and really setting oneself apart for potential business partners, investors, and even employers and employees: entrepreneurship.

The Young Entrepreneur: A Dwindling Species

Contrary to popular belief, we do not have a glut of new companies and entrepreneurship among America's youth. The noise from the startup scene aside, relatively *fewer* young people today are becoming their own bosses and launching their own enterprises. The percentage of young people who own private stock is at a low of 3.6%, down from 10.6% in 1989, according to the Wall Street Journal.[xlvi]

There are a few factors that play into this, but one of the most disempowering is student loan debt. While formal higher education and launching a business aren't mutually exclusive, it's particularly hard to make the sacrifices needed to launch a business early on when a grad is juggling paying back tens of thousands of dollars on a loan. Lifestyle inflation that results from a heavily subsidized pre-career at college with a multimillion dollar sports complex, free food on Fridays in the quad, and a variety of free or low-cost entertainment opportunities also contributes.

Apprenticeships For The 21st Century

Instead, a combination of high-discipline education and work experience serves a young person trying to set themselves apart best. They can combine the advantages of being educated in a variety of topics with the push given by the work-world to learn marketable skills. Rather than being insulated from the workforce for four years (on top of the twelve they spend as a youth), they can build their networks, learn new skills, and develop their own personal brand — all while receiving a quality education.

A revisiting of the apprenticeship model is one simple approach — entrepreneurs and business owners take promising young people under their wings and give them the opportunity to prove themselves. This not only provides the human capital benefits often spoken of in discussions about college (although rarely realized), but it can be done at a much lower cost to the young person by cutting out the bloated administrative costs and the federal subsidies system around higher education.

If our goal in discussions on education and career preparedness is to provide the best advice possible to promising young people, then continuing the "everybody who can go to college absolutely should in order to stay competitive" trope is one of the worst things we can do. Real discipline, skills, and education are better provided by marketplace actors who were forced to earn their wings than by those institutions that merely jump through accreditation hoops.

The End of this Book

The purpose of this book is not to sell you on anything. It's to explain, firsthand, my experiences with education and the evolution of my views. As I noted in the first chapter, too often we have people theorizing on education from the Ivory Tower or from their mom's basements. It's important to have somebody who is still what most people would consider (age-wise) "a student" explain education.

If you're wondering what I recommend you do after finishing this book, that depends on who you are.

Young People ("Students")

If you're currently enrolled in school, seriously ask yourself what you want to get out of your education. With the current setup of schooling, for some people, more school will be the right answer — but this set of people is *considerably* smaller than most people think. Unless you absolutely know you want to go into a highly-credentialed, legally restricted field (like practicing medicine as a doctor), then take time to discover exactly what you want to get out of your education.

The practical question you need to ask yourself is not "how do most people achieve what I want to achieve?" but rather, "what's the fastest, best, and cheapest way I can achieve what I want to achieve?" If you want to be a tech entrepreneur, you're better served by going and learning what it's like to start and run a tech company with somebody who's already done it. If you want to be a writer, you're best served by writing. If you want to be a scientist, you're best served by immersing yourself in the field.
There's an unhealthy pressure placed on young people to get the most prestigious credential they can reasonably get — even

when a considerably less prestigious one (or none!) would work just as well. Fight against this. Constantly remind yourself that your time is valuable and you are the one who ultimately decides how it is spent.

Also understand the key takeaway about the difference between "school" and "education" that I've offered here: most people go to school for a credential, not an education. If you pick up an education while you are there, that's a great, but secondary, effect of the credentialing process. If you think about school, education, and credentialing in these terms, it will help you to better understand the tradeoffs you face in your professional and educational life. It will help you avoid looking back on your school years and feeling gypped that you did not get the education you wanted.

If you aren't a parent yet but do plan on becoming one someday, please seriously consider what I've said here when your children come of school-age. With every year, alternatives to traditional schooling will become cheaper and more accessible — you won't need to have one parent stay at home without a career in order to give your child a great education outside of school. How you choose to let your children be educated is ultimately your call, but I urge you to seriously consider the points presented here.

Parents

Read the last paragraph of the "Young People" section. That applies to you, too. If you've ever been tempted to try out home education, *do it!* What's the worse that can happen? You spend some more time with your own flesh and blood and ultimately decide that it isn't best for you? Now you'd at least know.

I recommend Jeff Till's *Rise Above School* if you are seriously considering K-12 education outside of school. Jeff is a parent who decided only after-the-fact to home educate.

On the issue of higher education: understand that higher education is a credentialing service that comes with trade-offs. I've heard too many parents push their children, totally unprepared, into the expensive and time-consuming process that is college, usually telling them, "At least you'll have it under your belt!" or "It's a great way to find yourself!"

Not everybody who chooses not to get a Bachelor's degree is going to be a total burnout, stoned on the couch with greasy Dorito film on their fingers. In fact, they may even be more successful than their peers with degrees.

Success is a factor largely left up to the individual. The studies and reports you read about how having a degree is correlated with X measure of success is a consequence of a selection bias. Historically, harder working, more intelligent young people were more likely to attend college. It's these traits, not having the degree, that makes them more likely to be successful.

If your child decides they want to opt-out of school, approach it from an empathetic and supportive position. They're an adult and it is ultimately their call.

Educators

I hope by now you've realized that this not a book against you (the dedication is to two of my own teachers — two that helped save me from the stultifying effects of school in the era of No Child Left Behind). It is because I love education that I wrote this book.

Take what is said here and incorporate it into how you teach. Sometimes, the very best teachers are the ones that leave students to their own devices the most. Provide the resources and the environment necessary for young people to feed their curiosity — don't try to force a specific curiosity upon them.

If you have older students, help fight against the stigma associated with taking a gap year. It is much better for a young person to take a year and discover what they love (and hate!) and then choose what to do with their higher education after that than to throw an unprepared young person — even a smart one — who hasn't had any real experience with the world for the last 12 years into the costly and time-consuming pit that is college. If they discover that they need a degree to get where they want to go, they can go get it. There's no requirement that young people go to college immediately after high school. Understand that school is a tool for achieving a proper sense of education and that not all young people are meant for school — and that this includes smart, intelligent, hard-working young people! Far too often have I met educators who agree with me that "too many young people go to college/go to graduate school/take AP classes, etc." but they are approaching the issue from a fundamentally different perspective. Their perspective is that too many *low quality* young people are doing those things. Never mind the weird elitism caught in this sentiment, it's wrongheaded to think that high quality young talent is inherently driven towards and best served by school.

Employers

Finding strong talent is hard, I get that. I've spent the last few years finding good talent and sending it to quickly-growing firms and it is even hard for me — and that occupies most of my time! But by keeping a strong degree requirement, you are locking out good talent from your company and you are taking otherwise-great talent and requiring that they get loaded down by four years of less-than-ideal work and education and, oftentimes, a ton of debt.

It's no longer 1995! You can screen candidates digitally to find the best and you no longer have to place all this weight in the credential as a sorting mechanism. Many of the entrepreneurs I've worked with express to me that where a candidate gets a degree does not tell you much at all about the candidate.

Use technology. The disruption in higher education that has been happening over the past decade didn't come from delivery mechanisms like Udemy or Coursera — it came from signaling mechanisms like LinkedIn and Wordpress. Google is killing the credential — not MOOcs.

Remove the degree requirement — automatically screen out bad candidates based on things like response-time and writing ability. Open up the world to the end of school. Your company and your talent will be better off without the degree requirement.

Everybody Else

If you don't fall into any of the categories above, take what I've said here and communicate it to those in the above categories in your life. Understand that we were all young people once and have empathy for children and young adults. Don't subject them to things you yourself wouldn't want to be subjected to and don't advocate for subjecting them to these things.

Know that culture isn't something that any one central designer creates but is something that we all reinforce in our actions, biases, behavior, thinking, and even subconscious activities. Culture can't be changed with the waving of a wand but can be changed over generations. If you plan to have kids, know that the burden is on you to control their education, even if that means passively giving them up to your local compulsory government schools. If you are an uncle or an aunt, throw in your two cents about education. Let these ideas be heard. Let others mull them over and make decisions for themselves. Don't get caught up in the minutiae of reform but focus inwardly on that which you can control — your life and the lives dependent on you.

The end of school is coming. Are you prepared?

Further Reading

I have tried, throughout this book, to keep direct, academic-style citations to a minimum. This isn't solely for convenience — it's intentional. The writings in this book are the culmination of years of thought and experience — my own and others (see Acknowledgements for personal experiences).

The influences I've had on the topics of education, school, and work are many, and my personal philosophy on the matter spans subject matters — authors in sociology, philosophy, education reform, entrepreneurship and business, and economics all play an influence here. There's no common theme here — these aren't *all* books on education. They're just the books that influenced my thinking the most over the last few years.

These are just a few of the works and authors. You can find more of my influences on the topics of education and school at my blog, www.zakslayback.com. If you are interested in specific recommendations or just starting a conversation, please feel free to contact me at zak@slayback.xyz.

Nicomachean Ethics, Aristotle

> Happiness depends on ourselves.

Aristotle's idea of human flourishing — *eudaemonia* — is at the core of much of my thinking. The purpose of the human being's life is to strive towards flourishing and to strike virtues between vices. We use our rational faculties to work towards these ends, and the purpose of education is to give us the proper tools for these faculties to get to our personal conceptions of happiness. To live a happy life is not to feel persistent joy but rather to live virtuously and to always be working towards an end. Aristotle laid the groundwork for most of Western Philosophy but particularly for those focused on asking the question, "What does it mean to live happily?" I strongly recommend the *Nicomachean Ethics* to anybody interested in that question and related questions like, "What are virtues?" "What is the purpose of life?" and "What is happiness?" These are practical questions not to be ignored.

The Six Pillars of Self-Esteem, Branden, Nathaniel

> [L]ife is a process of self-generating and self-sustaining action.

Nathaniel Branden was a psychologist who followed in Aristotle's footsteps — focused on the question of what it means to live a happy life and how to get there. Influenced also by Ayn Rand, Branden eschews the Self-Esteem Movement that says everybody should get a trophy and emphasizes that self-esteem is not something that can come from others but must come from oneself. It comes from the individual knowing what his values are and acting in accordance with those values. This is the core of integrity and of self-esteem. Compulsory schooling crushes self-esteem in the youngest by connecting success to arbitrary factors like how well you can do long division. Schools crush self-efficacy, self-respect, and self-responsibility. The infantilization of young people stymies their abilities to develop a strong sense of self-esteem and their abilities to live happily. Branden goes step-by-step through the fundamentals of self-esteem and gives practical advice to parents, teachers, and those looking to get control over their self-esteem. If this is too much in the self-help vein for you, I recommend *The Psychology of Self-Esteem* or *The Psychology of Romantic Love*.

Flow: The Psychology of Optimal Experience, Csikszentmihalyi, Mihaly

> To overcome the anxieties and depressions of contemporary life, individuals must become independent of the social environment to the degree that they no longer respond exclusively in terms of its rewards and punishments. To achieve such autonomy, a person has to learn to provide rewards to herself. She has to develop the ability to find enjoyment and purpose regardless of external circumstances.

If you've ever sat down to work on something for a few minutes only to find that hours have passed, you've experienced flow. This is what Czikszentmihalyi calls "optimal experience" and this is strongly connected to what it takes to live a happy life and to work happily. Learning, reading, writing, doing work, creating art, and engaging in sports are all things that can cause us to fall into a state of flow, but these have to be voluntarily chosen by the individual. Being forced to work or to learn or to do anything cannot result in optimal experience. Play (see *Free to Learn*, below) is a core element of this process and play cannot, by definition, be imposed. Compulsory schooling removes much of the opportunity for the individual to develop the necessary psychological conditions to achieve flow and to do happy work. You probably remember the joy and playfulness with which you discovered new skills and knowledge as a child and wonder where that went. Most people just assume losing that is part of growing up but it doesn't have to be that way.

Weapons of Mass Instruction, Gatto, John Taylor

> We don't need state-certified teachers to make education happen — certification probably guarantees it won't.

Gatto has been called "hyperbolic" and "one-sided" but also "not wrong." His books are some of the best collections of first-hand accounts of the dangers of modern compulsory schooling and its effects on young people. He was New York's Teacher of the Year in 1991 and publicly quit in an op-ed to the *Wall Street Journal,* telling all that he can no longer do a job that "hurt[s] kids for a living." Gatto is no academic — do not expect rigorous citations and turning to academic papers. He tells his experiences with compulsory schooling through story and through history. His magnum opus, *The Underground History of American Education* is best for history buffs. The rest of his books are best for parents or students. Gaito asserts that the purpose of modern compulsory schooling is to make students indifferent, confused, accepting of their status in the world, emotionally and intellectually dependent, lack self-esteem, and feel like they're always being watched. This is one of the best works to really come to grips with the reality of modern schooling. As Gatto points out in the *Underground History,* this all sounds like a conspiracy — but the scary thing is that it isn't. If it were a conspiracy, it would have a simple solution. It's an amalgamation of cultural, personal, economic, and intellectual biases. Undoing these is a life-long process.

Free to Learn, Gray, Peter

> We have forgotten that children are designed by nature to learn through self-directed play and exploration, and so, more and more, we deprive them of freedom to learn, subjecting them instead to the tedious and painfully slow learning methods devised by those who run the schools.

Gray's work in *Free to Learn* is fundamental to understanding that education can and does happen outside of schools — and it can happen quite well. A research professor at Boston College, Gray explores the psychology and anthropology of education after his son comes to hate school. He pulls school, work, education, and play apart from each other and finds that human beings have evolved to learn through what we would think of today as unstructured, unsupervised "play" with no explicit educational ends. He goes further to show how compulsory schooling — whether private or public — teaches young people to view learning as a form of work and work as something tedious and not to be enjoyed. A good portion of the book focuses on his exploration of the Sudbury Valley School in Framingham, MA, and how you can create a schooling environment that is actually conducive to educating young people in a meaningful way. It turns out, if you leave young people to their own devices and give them the responsibility that comes with that, their world doesn't actually devolve into *Lord of the Flies*.

"Cosmos and Taxis," Hayek, F.A.

> Every organization in which the members are not mere tools of the organizer will determine by commands only the function to be performed by each member, the purposes to be achieved, and certain general aspects of the methods to be employed, and will leave the detail to be decided by the individuals on the basis of their respective knowledge and skills.

Although an economist, Hayek is really a social scientist all around. "Cosmos and Taxis" is a short essay that takes a look at different types of orders — designed and spontaneous — and the distribution of knowledge in these orders. Language, Hayek argues, is a good example of a spontaneous order. There are no central commanders designing every facet of a language. Language evolves based on the knowledge and needs of all the individuals using it. This applies to the vast majority of knowledge, not just language-based knowledge. To have a central order that commands what is and is not a way to learn or what is and is not open to evolution in a given subject matter is to limit the use of the individuals studying that subject matter. The fact that there are young people who graduate from school and have no ability to conceive of alternative ways of approaching problems is a testament to this issue. Understanding Hayek's insights into the importance of distributed, evolutionary systems is integral to understanding that knowledge is rarely something that can be set in stone and handed down. This is not to say that Hayek denies objective truth; rather, he recognizes that the experts on a matter may have imperfect understanding and access to the information necessary to grasp the subject fully.

Outwitting the Devil, Hill, Napoleon

> Teach children the danger of believing anything merely because their parents, religious instructors, or someone else says it is so.

Hill is well known for inventing much of the modern self-help genre with his book *Think and Grow Rich*. *Outwitting the Devil* is a lesser-known and only recently released look at the institutions that keep people from realizing their full potential. Hill's estate refused to release the book until after he had passed away out of fear that the criticisms of schools, government, and organized religion would spark backlash. Hill's central thesis is that there are certain forces in the world — he says used by "the Devil," but you can read into the mysticism as much or as little as you like and still get value out of the book — that keep people from achieving definiteness of purpose — or keeps them "drifting," as Hill says. People float through life without actually jumping into control of their own lives. They do what sparks the approval of others or what is expected of them — not what will help them live in accordance with their values. One of the big focuses is the effects that schools have on beating definiteness of purpose out of children. By setting up arbitrary goalposts and punishing failure, schools lead young people to seek out approval of authority figures — teachers or parents, usually — instead of focusing on the important question of "what is my own individual purpose?" This book is more in the self-help genre and is a good light read.

Deschooling Society, Illich, Ivan

> School is the advertising agency which makes you believe that you need the society as it is.

Illich's classic and radical *Deschooling Society* is a brief look at the effects that schooling have on society at large politically and economically. Modern schooling is integral to the economic makeup of crony corporatism and of the political institutions of the modern world. Despite being decades-old, *Deschooling Society* reads as if it were about the schools of today. Illich predicts a decentralized system of one-on-one, peer-to-peer education as a way forward as technology lowers the costs of connecting experts to people who want to learn (and for being written in 1971, that's a great prediction). Even if you don't agree with the political message of Illich's work, you can take valuable insights into the effects that centralized, compulsory schooling have on young people. Whether these are intentionally planned or perverse consequences — that's up to you.

"The Future of School," Morehouse, Isaac

> [S]chool is intended to provide universal basic skills and knowledge. In its quest to do so, it has become so regimented and programmed that it has shut out genuine confidence gained by experience. It has made learning a tedious chore of rote memorization, and divorced it from the real world of value to the learner.

This short booklet by Praxis founder and CEO Isaac Morehouse is a great answer to the question, "so, now what?" Breaking down the theory and the reality of higher education allows us to really see where school, especially in college, gets things wrong. Looking at how people learn best and how the resources available to us today allow for new, learner-driven attempts at education allows us to dispel of the myth that all intelligent, hard-working young people should go immediately into college. In fact, most great learning does not happen as a consequence of rote memorization in the classroom but as a consequence of immersion in the marketplace. (Full disclosure: at the time of this writing, I work with and am good friends with Isaac Morehouse — I still find this a valuable little booklet for somebody less interested in abstract theory and more interested in the "now what?")

Antifragile, Taleb, Nassim Nicholas

> Many people keep deploring the low level of formal education in the United states (as defined by, say, math grades). Yet these fail to realize that the new comes from here and gets imitated elsewhere. And it is not thanks to universities, which obviously claim a lot more credit than their accomplishments warrant. Like Britain in the Industrial Revolution, America's asset is, simply, risk taking and the use of optionality, this remarkable ability

> to engage in rational forms of trial and error, with no comparative shame in failing again, starting again, and repeating failure.

Antifragile is less about schooling or education and more about ways to think about systems and making decisions. Taleb, a risk analyst by trade, argues that some systems aren't just resistant to disorder, they actually *benefit* from it (i.e., rather than being fragile or robust, they are *antifragile*). Taleb argues we shouldn't look at probability of a high payoff as the core factor in making decisions but instead look at minimizing the downside. Education, too, can be antifragile and assuming that putting people through schools is the same thing as educating them not only prevents them from being able to reach their goals efficiently, it also offloads a lot of the downside on to the rest of society at large. Taleb's insistence on having skin in the game is powerful — don't argue for something if you're not willing to do it yourself and willing to risk getting burned if you're wrong. This is a delightful little book full of stories and ideas on everything from education and work to economics and nutrition.

Zero to One: Notes on Startups, or How to Build the Future, Thiel, Peter

> Elite students climb confidently until they reach a level of competition sufficiently intense to beat their dreams out of them. Higher education is the place where people who had big plans in high school get stuck in fierce rivalries with equally smart peers over conventional careers like management consulting and investment banking. For the privilege of being turned into conformists, students (or their families) pay hundreds of thousands of dollars in skyrocketing tuition that continues to outpace inflation.

> Why are we doing this to ourselves?

Peter Thiel is the philosopher king of Silicon Valley. The co-founder of PayPal and early investor in Facebook uses *Zero to One* (along with student and co-author Blake Masters) as an opportunity to decry the lack of definite, big-picture thinking in the West today and to give a roadmap for those who do want to build the future. Don't be fooled — this is not a book on business and entrepreneurship. This is a work of entrepreneurship, philosophy, social change, economics, political theory, and even a form of self-help. My top book in 2014, *Zero to One* is a must-read for any young person who is excited about going against the grain and interested in taking control of their own life. Most importantly, Thiel urges readers to not think of themselves as lottery tickets — you are not an aggregate or something left up to chance. Your education, your startup, and your career are all well within your control and you should not allow probabilities to stop you from undertaking new, ambitious projects. Thiel, a Stanford grad himself, decries elite education as an institution that dilutes the ambition of high-quality young people and feeds them into traditional careers like banking and law instead of inventing the future. This book was fundamental to putting into words many of my own intuitions and feelings on elite higher education.

Rise Above School, Till, Jeff

> The 15,000-hour decision is upon you: will you put your kids in the cinder-block cell of public school, or will you rescue them?

Jeff Till is an entrepreneur and a homeschool dad who wrote *Rise Above School* as an opportunity to educate and provide support for other parents considering pulling their children out of compulsory state schools. While *Rise Above School* does touch on the topics of the philosophy of state schooling and its history, the brief book is primarily practically oriented. The *magnum opus* of the book is the Complete Case for Home Education included within. Till moves step-by-step through all of the arguments he could devise when debating whether or not to pull his children from school and home educate them. He also identifies some of the long-term effects of a schooling regime, like the fact that children are expected to know what they want to be when they grow up despite never having actually worked a single day outside of schools.

Smart People Should Build Things, Yang, Andrew

> What's interesting is that many of the people I meet who are young, highly educated, and from good families are among the most risk-averse. They feel like they need to be making progress along a ladder with each passing month or year. Their parents have often set high expectations for them. They measure themselves each period against their peers, who are generally following various well-defined paths.

Andrew Yang is the founder of Venture For America, an organization that places recent college graduates in startups in cities that are not traditionally thought of as "startup cities." Yang is both a product of elite education and has worked with young people who are striving to get into elite schools. He saw firsthand the path dependency that drives smart, ambitious people into careers like law, medicine, banking, and consulting instead of starting projects and launching companies — building things. Yang founded Venture For America as an option for the ambitious college grad who isn't going to settle for a career that is expected of them and would rather go join a team that is actually building something. I can corroborate much of what Yang says affects ambitious young people today: they are risk-averse, they are always expected to be moving on a linear path set by each other and by parents, and they could be doing much more productive things with their careers and energies.

Endnotes:

[i] For more on the destructive nature of competition, see *Zero to One: Notes on Startups, Or How to Build The Future* by Peter Thiel and Blake Masters (Crown Business, 2014).

[ii] Full disclosure: the friend was Isaac Morehouse and the startup was Praxis, with whom I still work.

[iii] *http://www.paulgraham.com/top.html*

[iv] For more on the idea of mimetic theory, visit *www.imitatio.org*

[v] *Zero to One*, 68-69.

[vi] For more, see: *http://zakslayback.com/2015/04/01/the-steve-jobs-fallacy-of-opting-out-of-college/*

[vii] For hacking failure, see: *https:/medium.com/on-breaking-the-mold/failure-is-overrated-hacking-failure-for-success-e7b0c08591f9*

[viii] See: *http://www.usnews.com/education/blogs/the-college-solution/2011/03/01/the-ivy-league-earnings-myth*

[ix] Chalabi, Mona. "American Kids Will Spend An Average Of 943 Hours In Elementary School This Year." DataLab. Five Thirty Eight, 04 Sept. 2014. Web. 30 Mar. 2016.

[x] Gray, Peter. "Sonnet to a Playful God." *Psychology Today*. 04 Dec. 2014. Web. 27 Apr. 2016.

[xi] Jayson, Sharon. "Who's Feeling Stressed? Young Adults, New Survey Shows." USA Today. Gannett, 07 Feb. 2013. Web. 30 Mar. 2016.

[xii] Morehouse, Isaac. "Good Enough for a Dog? - Isaac Morehouse." Isaac Morehouse. 29 May 2013. Web. 30 Mar. 2016.

[xiii] Yang, Andrew. "The Six Paths of the Typical US College Graduate-and Why They're All Wrong." Quartz. 26 Sept. 2014. Web. 30 Mar. 2016.

[xiv] Weissmann, Jordan. "53% of Recent College Grads Are Jobless or Underemployed—How?" The Atlantic. Atlantic Media Company, 23 Apr. 2012. Web. 30 Mar. 2016.

[xv] "State by State Data." The Institute For College Access and Success. n.d. Web. 30 Mar. 2016.

[xvi] Peralta, Eyder. "AP Analysis: Half Of Recent College Grads Are Jobless Or Underemployed." NPR. NPR, 23 Apr. 2012. Web. 31 Mar. 2016.

[xvii] Vedder, Richard. "Twelve Inconvenient Truths about American Higher Education." Center For College Affordability and Productivity. CCAP, Mar. 2012. Web.

[xviii] Jacobs, Peter. "There Are Now 50 Colleges That Charge More Than $60,000 Per Year." Business Insider. Business Insider, Inc, 10 July 2014. Web. 31 Mar. 2016.

[xix] Staton, Michael. "The Degree Is Doomed." Harvard Business Review. Harvard Business, 08 Jan. 2014. Web. 31 Mar. 2016.

[xx] Hanford, Emily. "Rethinking the Way College Students Are Taught." American RadioWorks. American Public Media, 2016. Web. 31 Mar. 2016.

[xxi] Altman, Sam. "Advice for Ambitious 19 Year Olds." Sam Altman. 24 June 2013. Web. 31 Mar. 2016.

[xxii] Refer to Endnote 10

[xxiii] De Avila, Joseph. "Crane Operators Top $500,000 in Pay, Benefits." WSJ. The Wall Street Journal, 25 June 2011. Web. 31 Mar. 2016.

[xxiv] "10 Highest-Paying Jobs That Don't Require A Bachelor's Degree." AOL.com. AOL., 15 May 2014. Web. 31 Mar. 2016.

[xxv] Berman, Jillian. "Class of 2015 Has the Most Student Debt in U.S. History." MarketWatch. MarketWatch, 9 May 2015. Web. 31 Mar. 2016.

[xxvi] Refer to Endnote 10
[xxvii] O'Shaughnessy, Lynn. "The Ivy League Earnings Myth." The College

Solution. US News, 1 Mar. 2011. Web. 31 Mar. 2016.

[xxviii] Onink, Troy. "Unless You're Average, College ROI And Best Value Rankings Are Misleading." Forbes. Forbes Magazine, 31 July 2015. Web. 31 Mar. 2016.

[xxix] Refer to Endnote 20

[xxx] "U.S. Job Growth Expected to Hold Steady in the New Year, CareerBuilder's Annual Job Forecast Finds - CareerBuilder." Careerbuilder. CareerBuilder, 9 Oct. 2014. Web. 31 Mar. 2016.

[xxxi] Sherriff, Lucy. "Ernst & Young Removes Degree Classification From Entry Criteria As There's 'No Evidence' University Equals Success." The Huffington Post UK. Huffington Post, 18 Jan. 2016. Web. 31 Mar. 2016.

[xxxii] Wakabayashi, Daisuke. "College Dropouts Thrive in Tech." WSJ. Wall Street Journal, 3 June 2015. Web. 31 Mar. 2016.

[xxxiii] Bessen, James. "Employers Aren't Just Whining – the." Harvard Business Review. Harvard Business, 25 Aug. 2014. Web. 31 Mar. 2016.

[xxxiv] Rampell, Catherine. "The College Degree Has Become the New High School Degree." Washington Post. The Washington Post, 9 Sept. 2014. Web. 31 Mar. 2016.

[xxxv] Simon, Ruth. "Endangered Species: Young U.S. Entrepreneurs." WSJ. Wall Street Journal, 2 Jan. 2015. Web. 31 Mar. 2016.

[xxxvi] Sparshott, Jeffrey. "Congratulations, Class of 2015. You're the Most Indebted Ever (For Now)." WSJ. Wall Street Journal, 8 May 2015. Web. 31 Mar. 2016.

[xxxvii] Ambrose, Brent W., Larry Cordell, and Shuwei Ma. "The Impact of Student Loan Debt on Small Business Formation*." PhiladelphiaFED. Working Papers, July 2015. Web. 31 Mar. 2016.

[xxxviii] Schoenberger, Chana. "Want to Be an Entrepreneur? Beware of Student Debt." WSJ. Wall Street Journal, 26 May 2015. Web. 01 Apr. 2016.

[xxxix] Shane, Scott. "Is Student Debt the Reason Millennials Aren't Starting Companies?" Entrepreneur. Entrepreneur Media, 03 Aug. 2015. Web. 01 Apr. 2016.

[xl] Shane, Scott. "Are Millennials Really the Entrepreneurial Generation?" Entrepreneur. Entrepreneur Media, 04 Feb. 2014. Web. 01 Apr. 2016.

[xli] Zinshteyn, Mikhail. "The Skills Gap: America's Young Workers Are Lagging Behind." The Atlantic. Atlantic Media Company, 17 Feb. 2015. Web. 01 Apr. 2016.

[xlii] Urban, Tim. "Why Generation Y Yuppies Are Unhappy - Wait But Why." Wait But Why. Wait But Why, 2013. Web. 01 Apr. 2016.

[xliii] Russolillo, Steven. "Chart of the Day: Millennials Are Really Risk Averse." WSJ. Wall Street Journal, 29 May 2014. Web. 01 Apr. 2016.

[xliv] Rogers, Kate. "Millennials Most Risk Averse Generation Since Depression Era." Fox Business. Fox, 29 Jan. 2014. Web. 01 Apr. 2016.

[xlv] Stanley, Thomas J. "BLOG." Millionaires Reflections on High School Comments. Thomas J Stanley, 16 Nov. 2010. Web. 01 Apr. 2016.

[xlvi] Refer to Endnote 28

Made in the USA
Middletown, DE
11 July 2016